ROBINS

ROBINS
•CHRIS MEAD•

with illustrations by
KEVIN BAKER

Whittet Books

First published 1984
Reprinted 1989

Text © 1984 by Chris Mead
Illustrations © 1984 by Kevin Baker

Whittet Books Ltd, 113 Westbourne Grove, London W2 4UP

Design by John Saunders

British Library Cataloguing in Publication Data

Mead, Chris
  Robins.
  1. Robins
  I. Title
  598.8'42   QL696.P2
  ISBN 0-905483-36-7

To all Robin enthusiasts,
but particularly David Lack who showed us all
the way to Field Orthinology.

Acknowledgments
My profoundest debt is, of course, to the late David Lack who, with his studies of the Robin, was the first person in Britain to really get to grips with what makes a bird tick. His interest spread to all aspects of the Robin and not just the bald biological facts. His wife, Elizabeth, and son, Peter (currently a colleague of mine at the BTO), have been very helpful. It has been a pleasure to work again with Kevin Baker as illustrator. The British Section of the ICBP were a great help in finding out about the process by which the Robin became our national bird. David Harper told a little of the revelations he will be making about the private lives of his Robins in his forthcoming book. Many other colleagues at Beech Grove helped me in various ways but, as so often happens, much of this book could not have been written without the recorded observations published by dozens of amateur bird-watchers over the years gone by.

Formal acknowledgments
The Atlas map for Robins appears by permission of T & AD Poyser and the British Trust for Ornithology.

also in this series

HEDGEHOGS by Pat Morris

Typesetting by Columns
Printed and bound in Great Britain at the University Printing House, Oxford

Contents

Introduction

There is no other wild bird, in Britain, so much loved as the Robin. Throughout the country there are people who have a very special, personal, relationship with *their* Robin. Most do not realize it is they who have been chosen by the Robin, in setting up his or her territory: however, the special feeling which then may develop between Human and bird is mutual and may last for years.

In this book I have been able to document many aspects of the Robin's life, facts and figures about populations and migrations, nesting and feeding, life and death. This is also a book about our own reactions to the bird and so legends, nursery rhymes, religion and, above all, the Robin's tameness also feature. This makes the book terribly British for, although the map below shows that Robins as a species are very widely distributed, it is a fact that it is only *our* Robins that regularly confide in Humans.

July 1984   *Chris Mead, Tring*

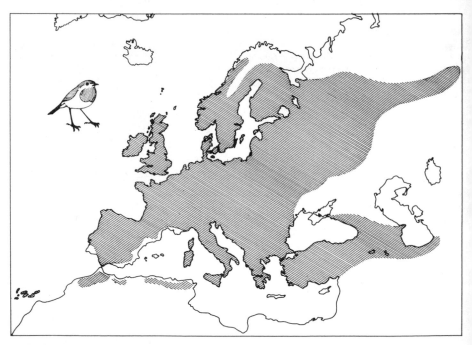

The shaded area is where Robins are regularly found breeding. It contains tracts of unsuitable country where Robins may be absent or very rare but, if there were suitable areas present, Robins would undoubtedly be there.

Distribution

The breeding distribution of the Robin stretches from the Azores in the west to Novosibirsk on the eastern edge of the West Siberian Plain. They reach beyond the Arctic circle to the north and there are resident populations in North Africa and the Canary Islands. The map shows the extent of Robinland although, of course, there may be unsuitable bits within the area where no Robins breed. The southern boundary roughly ends where the average temperature in July exceeds 23°C (73°F). The coasts of the Mediterranean are too hot for breeding Robins but the cooler mountains of North Africa contain a good deal of suitable habitats. In the north the boundary ends where summers are too cold, with average July temperatures less than 13°C (55°F). The map also shows the lack of breeding Robins in the cold mountains down the spine of Scandinavia.

Within Britain and Ireland the Robin is found as a breeding bird almost everywhere. The British Trust for Ornithology (BTO) did work for a breeding bird atlas between 1968 and 1972 and proved that of the 3,862 units that they monitored (each unit 10km by 10km) Robins were breeding in 3,503 of them. There were another 82 which probably or possibly held breeding Robins. Since every recording unit (defined by the National Grid lines) with any land in it was surveyed, there were quite a number of coastal squares with such tiny bits of land in them that they contained no suitable Robin habitat. The major areas from which Robins were missing included the tops of the main mountain ranges in Scotland, the whole of Shetland, most of Orkney and the Outer Hebrides and almost all of the exposed small island groups off the west coasts of Scotland and

Ireland. Planting of trees over the last 150 years has led to a gradual increase in breeding numbers on Orkney and the Outer Hebrides (and perhaps in the uplands of England, Wales and Scotland). Migrants (see p. 28) can often be found during the autumn and spring in many of the places without breeding birds: especially on Orkney, Shetland and the other northern islands of Scotland.

More detailed local breeding surveys in south-east England, based on smaller recording units called 'tetrads' (squares with sides 2km long), have shown just how widely distributed Robins are. The survey of the London area found Robins in 93% of the tetrads within 20 miles of St Paul's, including 14 of the 24 innermost ones. Breeding birds were present in various urban parks and gardens, including Buckingham Palace. In Hertfordshire, with virtually 100% coverage, Robins were found in 501 of 504 tetrads. The three misses were all on the chalky farmland area in the north-east of the county. Here the very large fields have few, if any, hedges and there is so little cover available that Robins really were absent. Most of the 34 records of birds seen but not proved or suspected to be breeding were from similar areas. In Kent the tetrad survey showed that Robins were absent from some stretches of the North Kent Marshes and most of the shingle expanse of Dungeness. Inland gaps also coincided with prairie farmland. In all these counties breeding was proved for all the units (10km × 10km) of the national survey.

Breeding bird atlas surveys carried out abroad are often based on a variety of different recording block sizes, but the Robin usually figures large no matter how the study has been constructed. In France (Corsica included) there were records from 96% of units; most of those missing Robins being along the Mediterranean coast. For Holland the score was 85% – birds were missing from some of the intensively cultivated areas and the exposed coastal sites. In Denmark 82% of the recording units had Robins – again they were missing from coastal sites in particular. Finally the Swiss survey had a 98% coverage for Robins, with the birds only missing from the highest parts of the Alps – breeding was proved up to 2,100m above sea level (nearly 6,500ft: half as high again as Ben Nevis).

During the autumn and winter even the local Robins within Britain may move around and so be found in areas where they are few and far between during the breeding season. In Europe largely the northern parts of the breeding range are deserted in the winter and migrant Robins spill off the southern edge of the breeding area into most of North Africa. They even go down to some of the northern oases of the Sahara and also far down the Nile Valley. The pattern of their movements is described on page 21. Migrant Robins are regularly found in the spring well to the north of the breeding range because they have overshot their target area on the return migration. Such birds have been recorded from the Faeroes, Iceland and even Jan Mayen but have never been known to stay and breed in these remote and unsuitable places: cold and with hardly any or no trees.

In The Times, *January 4th, 1984, we read of 'an 86-year-old woman who was admitted as an emergency just after Christmas 1981 to a Stockport hospital. She had been vomiting for a couple of days and had severe abdominal pain. Mr Edward Kiff reports the tale in a recent issue of the* British Medical Journal. *He operated on her and discovered the wall of her intestine had been punctured. Imagine his surprise when he examined the wound more closely and found it had been caused by the beak of a small plastic robin which had been part of her Christmas cake decoration. She made an uneventful recovery after the bird was removed.'*

Robin variations

Our own Robin is uniquely identified to ornithologists throughout the world by the name *Erithacus rubecula*. This is the scientific name for the species Robin which was designated by Linnaeus when he started to classify all the different bird species. The original Robin he named came from Sweden, near Stockholm, and over the years avian taxonomists (the people who study variation and classification in birds) have named a number of sub-species.

The species includes all birds that are expected to breed together in the wild in a continuous sweep over the species' entire range. The sub-species (given a third Latin name) are variations within this continuous range and generally are distinctive populations of breeding birds that are bigger, smaller, darker or lighter and can therefore be consistently distinguished from other populations. Since the Swedish birds were the first to be named, their sub-specific name is simply the species name repeated – they are thus *Erithacus rubecula rubecula*.

This is the race (another name for sub-species) which is found over most of Europe from the Atlantic in the west to the Urals in the east. This huge range is in part explained by the continuous mixing within the area brought about by the extensive migratory movements of this population which ensures a thorough mixing of the birds.

The main variation within the different Robin populations takes the form of 'clines' — continuous but gradual changes: the differences between birds from neighbouring places are imperceptible but they may be very marked for birds from far apart. For instance the grey-backed and lighter orange-breasted birds from mid-Europe become darker — the backs more olive and the breasts richer orange — to the west. Our own birds are *Erithacus rubecula melophilus* (meaning 'sweet singer') and get even darker in Ireland and Scotland than in the south-east of England. The same colour changes also take place southwards through Iberia and then eastwards through the western part of North Africa. The race from Tunisia (*Erithacus rubecula witherbyi*) looks identical to *E.r. melophilus* but is significantly smaller: these are two races (distinct populations) on the western and southern edges of the main area of distribution of the whole species.

The eastern race, *E.r. tataricus*, from Western Siberia is the palest of all. Running to the south-east in Asia is a different cline which also gives rise to darker birds: these also have rufous (a warm reddish tinge) on the upper-tail coverts. This is most pronounced in northern Iran where the local race is called *E.r. hyrcanus*. The birds here are as dark and richly coloured on the breast as the isolated race, *E.r. superbus*, which is found far away in the central islands of the Canaries, off the West African coast. The eastern islands of this group have birds identical to typical *E.r. rubecula*. It has been suggested that these are the offspring of a recent colonization but that the birds which gave rise to *superbus* have been on the Canaries for much longer.

Other Robins

Throughout the world, a large number of birds are called robins. Some are very closely related to our own but others are from different families and have been given the name robin only because they have red on the breast or behave like our familiar bird. For example the Pekin Robin (illustrated below) is actually a babbler (a tropical group of songbirds) and only distantly related to our bird. However it is a popular cage bird well known for its tame and confiding behaviour and also has a splash of red below the yellow on its upper breast. It comes from eastern Asia, including China, and has been imported as the Pekin Robin for a very long time. Its scientific name is *Leiothrix lutea* and it is a member of the Tamiliinae, a sub-family containing about 250 species of which none have been recorded naturally in the wild in Britain.

The Pekin Robin, Leiothrix lutea, *is best known in Europe as a popular cage bird.*

The American Robin is a completely different bird with a rather unfortunate name: *Turdus migratorius*. This is about the size of our Blackbird, also a *Turdus* – *Turdus merula*, and affectionately known by some ornithologists as 'the merry turd' – but has a distinctive orange breast and was therefore named Robin by the early settlers. As one would expect from its scientific name it is highly migratory, unlike 'ours', and retreats from the northern parts of its range in Canada and winters southwards into Mexico. Young birds are spotty breasted with a pale eyestripe – the adults have a pale ring round the eye. The bird's behaviour is very like our Blackbird's and it is held in great affection. Through an association with this species its close relative, *Turdus grayi*, another thrush from Mexico and Central America, has also been given the name robin. This is called the 'Clay-colored Robin' and is very like a slightly scaled down and marginally lighter version of our Blackbird – but completely lacking any red!

Even less related to our bird are the robins and robin-flycatchers of Australasia, New Guinea and the islands of Micronesia. These are closely related to our flycatchers and like them resemble our Robin in size and shape – some species are also very tolerant of man. Most of the species behave like

The American Robin, Turdus migratorius, *is as big as our Blackbird.*

flycatchers and catch their food during short flights from a vantage point but some actually feed on the ground like 'our' Robin. Several also have patches of red on their breasts — for example the Scarlet Robin-flycatcher, *Petroica multicolor*, which is an Australian species. This bird has striking black and white upperparts, a black head and white forehead and glorious scarlet throat, breast and belly. Close relatives include many with yellow rather than red on the breast but others have pale lilac or rose colours. In New Zealand the native Robin, *Petroica australis*, is a dark grey bird with paler underparts and a conspicuous white forehead spot. It is found in woodland and behaves very like the European Robin.

In parts of Australia and New Guinea there are two species of scrub-robins which are thought to be members of the thrush family. The one illustrated is the Northern Scrub-robin, *Drymodes supercilliaris*, which is rather like the southern European Rufous Bush-chat, *Cercotrichas galactotes*, with a long, broad tail with white on the tips of the outer feathers. The bush-chat is sometimes put in the same genus as the scrub-robins of Africa. Two are illustrated: the White-winged, *Erythropygia leucoptera*, and the Eastern Bearded *E. quadruvirigata*. Both are from the central part of Eastern Africa. Although it is usual for these birds to be classified with the thrushes and close to the European Robin there is some doubt and they may best be put with the babblers. All have the same habits and feed a great deal on the ground. They are generally found in rather dry, scrubby and bushy areas. They are often very

The Northern Scrub Robin, Drymodes supercilliaris, *comes from Australia.*

The White-winged Scrub Robin, Erythropygia leucoptera *(left) and the Eastern Bearded Scrub Robin,* E. quadruvirigata *(right) are both from East Africa.*

difficult to see and the most obvious thing about them is their 'tchacks' of alarm at any intruder.

Another exotic 'robin' is the Magpie Robin, *Copsychus saularis*, of south-east Asia. This is quite a close relative of the Robin with similar habits and shape. It is a bit bigger and its plumage is black and white (see illustration) in the male, dark grey and white in the female. New settlers in the Far East discovered this bird as a tame companion in their gardens, just like the garden Robin at home. What more appropriate name for a black-and-white robin than Magpie Robin?

South-east Asia is the home of the Magpie Robin, Copsychus saularis.

There remain the close relatives of our own Robin, *Erithacus rubecula*. Most taxonomists currently agree that there is only one species in the genus *Erithacus* although some add the Japanese and Ryukyu Robins, *E. akahige* and *E. komadori*. These two are illustrated – the former is found all over Japan and on the Soviet island of Sakhalin to the north, the latter only on the Ryukyu islands, which are between Japan to the north and Taiwan to the south. The female Japanese Robin is very like ours but the orange does not extend so far down the bird's front; the male has the same amount of orange as the female

The Japanese Robin, Erithacus akahige, *is our Robin's closest relative.*

The male Ryukyu Robin, Erithacus komadori, *has a black breast.*

The Siberian Rubythroat, Luscinia calliope.

and a grey lower breast and flanks. In the more southerly species the orange is completely absent and replaced by a black forehead, throat and upper breast in the male and by a pale breast with faint brown bars in the female. These birds are very similar in size, shape and habit to our birds but are separated from them by several thousand kilometres. In the intervening area the Robin's place in the local bird community is occupied by the Siberian Rubythroat, *Luscinia calliope.* This bird has a superb red throat with two white stripes on each side of the head and a white eyestripe. It is an exceptionally rare vagrant to Europe.

Other robin-like birds include our own Nightingale, *Luscinia megarhynchos,* which is a bit bigger and lacks any red on the underparts – though it has a strong rufous wash on its tail. It and its very close relative the Sprosser, *L. luscinia,* are found to the south of the Robin's range and in its southern half. To the north, and in its northern half, Bluethroats, *Luscinia svecica,* breed. Very much the same shape and size as a Robin, they have blue instead of orange throats (although some races have red central patches); they also have red sides to the mid-tail. Nightingales breed in small numbers in south-eastern England,

A male White-spotted form of Bluethroat, Luscinia svecica — *a rare migrant in Britain.*

whereas Bluethroats are rare passage migrants generally seen along the east coast in autumn.

Two further species must be mentioned. The first is the Red-flanked Bluetail, *Tarsiger cyanurus*, which breeds from Kamchatka in the North Pacific westwards to eastern Finland. Another very rare vagrant to Britain (its normal migration is eastwards to south-east Asia), it is clearly a close relative of the Robin and a very few aberrant Robins have been found closely resembling this species (see page 17). Finally Philip Guille, a ringer on Sark in the Channel Islands, was amazed on October 27th, 1975, to catch a slightly larger but short-tailed robin. Detailed research showed this to be the first record for Europe of the Siberian Blue Robin, *Luscinia cyane*, whose normal breeding area starts north of the Himalayas and spreads eastwards to include Japan! The birds normally migrate south eastwards into China, the Philippines and even reach as far as Borneo; Heaven knows what it was doing on Sark, although that autumn produced large numbers of very rare birds from Siberia in Western Europe — so the weather was certainly at least partly to blame.

Robin introductions

Since the Robin is such a favourite at home it is not surprising that there have been numerous attempts by human immigrants to introduce it to foreign countries as part of an attempt to make the people's new home like the one they left behind. In fact there were many *Acclimatization Societies* set up in the middle of the last century to promote the introduction of European birds to Australia and New Zealand in particular. For the Robin attempts were made near Melbourne (Australia) and in various parts of New Zealand, as well as in Canada and at least five places in the United States of America. All the attempts failed and in most cases the birds were hardly seen at all after their release.

The Robin – 'introduced' all over the world.

Whatever the motives of the people who sought to introduce the Robins and other birds to new countries the results were generally disastrous. Either, as in the case of the Robins, their attempts failed and the introduced birds died; or, even worse in many respects, some species of introduced birds thrived and competed with the local populations. For instance, Starlings were among the birds introduced in many places. As their numbers built up they began to compete successfully against the local species for cavity nesting places. Being resourceful and aggressive, Starlings generally win such contests and this reduced the numbers of local bird populations, and they swiftly made a dramatic takeover. In fact the Starling has been one of the most successful newcomers to the USA and spread across the entire North American continent in the space of only half a century. By comparison, the Robin has been a complete failure as a colonizer, despite being given plenty of encouragement.

Both the closest relatives of our Robin, the Japanese and the Ryukyu Robins, have also been the subject of introduction attempts; this time on Hawaii, but with little success. The former was established for some years on Oahu but is not known to be there now. The fate of the latter is unknown.

With 'our' Robin the odds were stacked firmly against any successful introduction. First of all the birds had to endure a long sea voyage, whether they

Starlings have found no difficulty in establishing breeding populations in many parts of the world to which they have been introduced.

were going to America or Australasia. If their destination was in the southern hemisphere their internal clock would be totally disrupted by an unnatural crossing of the equator. Conditions in their cages cannot have been good for a species which is normally solitary and territorial. The newly arrived birds may not have been in a very good condition when they were released into alien surroundings. The voyage must have lasted several weeks; they might even have been seasick. On top of all these problems it is quite likely that the sex ratio of the imported birds was heavily biased towards males — they are more likely to have been caught by the bird-catchers, who supplied the birds, than females!

Still, it's a bit surprising that the Robin did not at least hold its own in New Zealand. That country had no native predatory mammals to cause trouble, plenty of insect food and a moderate climate. Lots of other British birds actually did rather well there and are more commonly seen than New Zealand species. However, perhaps it is significant that most of the successful bird immigrants to New Zealand are gregarious seed-eaters like the Greenfinch or Goldfinch. Maybe Robins were introduced in small numbers, dispersed and failed to find mates or enough food? Maybe New Zealand's own Robin took a dim view of this immigrant competitor and outsmarted it — who knows? But if the Robin could not establish itself in the comparatively sheltered conditions of New Zealand it's scarcely surprising that it was unable to thrive in the USA or Australia.

Aberrant Robins

There are two sorts of *strange* Robins that are most often seen: birds with physical deformities and those with plumage abnormalities. Of these the cases of albino or partially albino birds are most easily explained.

Albino birds are individuals that have pigment lacking from part or all of the plumage and therefore appear white in parts or all over. In addition there are what are properly known as 'leucistic' birds, whose plumage colour is very diluted; these are often also (incorrectly) known as albinos. Fully albino birds rarely survive since the loss of pigment from all parts of the bird not only makes them very conspicuous (and thus likely to be seen and caught by predators). In addition, albinism results in a lack of pigment in the eyes (making them pink) and this affects the bird's power of sight. However apparently complete albinos — with totally white plumage, pink eyes, legs and beaks — have been occasionally found in the wild.

Albinism is not particularly common in Robins although there are a fair number of birds recorded with just a few white feathers — generally round the head. Other variations include grey-backed birds with normal orange underparts, pale biscuit-coloured birds lacking any red and totally speckled

Albino Robins are not very common and pure white birds, like this one, have little chance of survival in the wild.

birds with white spotting over the whole plumage. In many species albinism runs in particular groups of birds in a small area (presumably closely related individuals sharing the same 'whiteness' genes) but this does not often seem to happen with Robins. Also there are only a few records of progressive albinism affecting a few feathers on a bird and gradually becoming more widespread as the bird grows older and undergoes further moults. Again, this is a feature more often recorded in other species: in Britain, particularly male Blackbirds.

Xanthochroism is a phenomenon that results in a yellow bird. It is very rare and again caused by genes. It has only once been recorded in British Robins by ringers in Yorkshire who caught three different birds in the summers of 1976, 1977 and 1978. All were ringed, so it was not the same bird involved each time and, in any case, all three birds were juveniles. The birds were generally a pale orange-yellow throughout — even their soft parts; perhaps they had been eating too many carrots, or had a nasty attack of jaundice.

Other plumage variations are of a very interesting nature for the birds have shown plumage features very like two of their close relatives. In three instances

The only time an albino Robin is not conspicuous — after heavy snow.

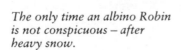

(South Wales, Yorkshire and Cheshire) features of the aberrant birds included blue on the breast like in a Bluethroat (*Luscinia svecica*). In the other three cases, two from Cape Clear in County Cork and a single bird in Norfolk, the birds had a very close resemblance to a Red-flanked Bluetail (*Tarsiger cyanurus*). The juvenile Red-flanked Bluetail is very like a Robin, but the adult male is blue above, with orange flanks and creamy underparts. The aberrant birds were like females or immatures with olive-brown upperparts, a blue flush over the rump and tail and a warm orange flush on the flanks. Several observers were almost wholly fooled by these birds, the first of which was trapped by ringers and turned out, for certain, to be a 'funny' Robin. This aberration seems to have been mainly caused by lack of red pigment although some was still present on parts of the underparts giving a pale russet wash to the plumage.

Physical deformity seems almost always to be the result of damage or injury. Most inherited deformities would be too serious a burden for a bird to survive and so any congenitally deformed chicks would fail to fledge. However, as I write this, I have a Robin resident in my garden that has elongated and crossed upper and lower parts of its beak. It seems to feed itself well and has maintained a reasonable weight all winter. Its deformity may have been started by suffering a broken beak by flying against a window but it may have been inherited. There is a record of a pair of Robins, including one with a crossed bill, producing youngsters of which one had the same defect. This shows that genetic sources of such aberrations cannot always be discounted.

Habitat

The Robin was originally a bird of the mature deciduous forests of Europe. In these a rich mixture of trees grew to prodigious heights with a thick layer of undergrowth below them. A natural part of the life of these forests was the toppling of over-mature trees. Whilst new saplings struggled to take advantage of the gap in the canopy, this created substantial glades, which were particularly favoured by pairs of Robins. However, many also bred successfully under the closed tree canopy. Even then Robins were not confined to the forests for they also existed on the forest edges and in heathland and wooded fenland areas. Unfortunately we cannot see Robins in Britain breeding in unspoilt mature natural woods: the only place where such forests still exist is on the Polish/Soviet border in the magnificent Bialowieza forest.

What all these habitats have in common are areas of thick, low cover. This is the essential component of any place in which the Robin will make its home. Robins are adapted to feed on the ground or by dropping to the ground from a low perch to collect a food item. Since they are territorial for most of the year they also need song-posts to advertise their territorial boundaries. Species that live in open habitats are generally gregarious: the chance of spotting a predator is so much better if there are many pairs of eyes to spot its arrival. In dense shrubbery, such as the Robin prefers, there are plenty of places to hide and no need of 'safety in numbers'.

The Robin has increased greatly in numbers over the last few thousand years, for the changes in habitat brought about by man, particularly in Britain, have made many more suitable areas in which the Robin can breed. Within the primeval forests, if the Polish reserves are anything to go by, the Robin was a very widespread but rather sparsely distributed bird. In most of Britain's woodlands today there are fewer large trees and more young trees with thick undergrowth – ideal of Robins. In farmland areas the small copses, often left for gamebirds or foxes, are also ideal, as are the thicker hedges and areas along the woodland edge.

However, it is now around our buildings that Robins are most familiar. For instance there can be few churchyards without at least one pair of resident Robins and many larger ones will have several. Huge numbers breed in gardens of all kinds – ranging from the ones around isolated farmhouses, those in villages, country towns, suburbia and even right in the middle of the biggest cities. It is human nature to want to arrange one's garden with shrubs and hedges ensuring a degree of privacy – and this is just what the breeding Robin needs too. During the winter the same Robins are helped by the millions of people who put out food for the birds: this has cemented the relationship – some would say it has almost become dependence.

It was not always like this; there are references from the sixteenth century that indicate that the Robin was predominantly a winter visitor to the vicinity of houses. For example in 1678 John Ray wrote of the Robin:

> In Winter-time to seek food it enters into houses with much confidence, being a very bold bird, sociable and familiar with man. In the summer time (as *Turner* saith) when there is plenty of food in the Woods, and it is not pinched with cold, it withdraws itself with its Brood into the most desert places.

Turner was writing in 1544, well over a century before Ray. However the tradition of gardening, in the way that we now know it, developed through the eighteenth and nineteenth centuries and by Victorian times the Robin was a familiar garden breeding bird and not one that abandoned the garden in favour of woodland in the spring time.

Over much of the rest of Europe the pattern of land use has not produced the British mosaic of fields, small woodlands and thick hedges. Nor, until recently, has there been a similar tradition of gardening around the homes for such a high proportion of the human population. This has led to their Robins being rather rarer than in Britain and largely confined to habitats approaching the wholly 'natural' ones where the birds would have been found centuries ago. In this respect, the Robin as we know it is very much a British bird, a special part of our heritage which has evolved hand-in-hand with our distinctive traditional landscape.

Migration

To most people in Britain the very idea of Robins migrating probably seems
absurd. They always seem to be here, and the only time of the year when we
miss our garden Robin is the short period in the late summer when the birds

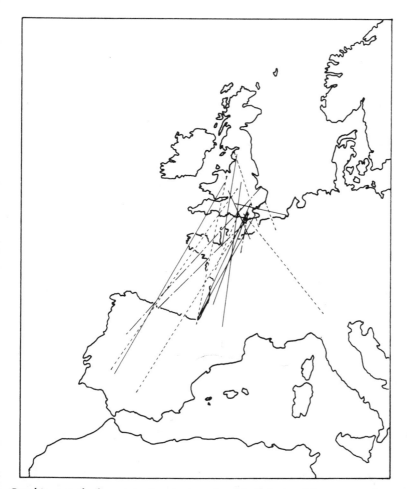

*On this map the lines join the ringing places in Britain with recovery places
abroad. In all cases the Robins were of British origin:*
  Solid lines – ringed as nestlings
  Dotted lines – as juveniles in the breeding season
  Broken lines – as adults in the breeding season

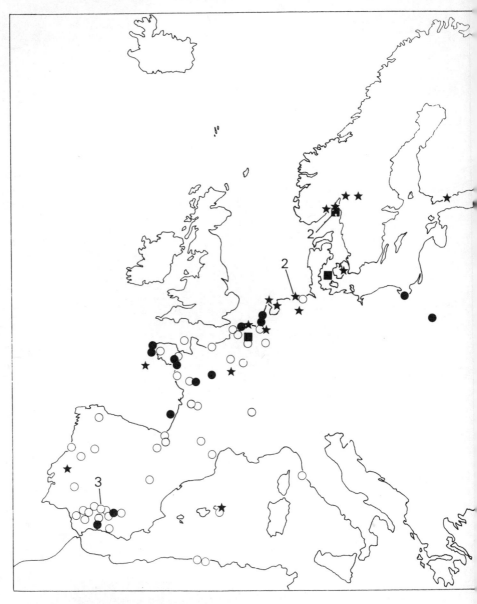

The finding places abroad of young birds ringed in Britain in the autumn.
The season of recovery is shown by the symbol:

  Star – spring   Square – summer
  Black dot – autumn   Circle – winter.

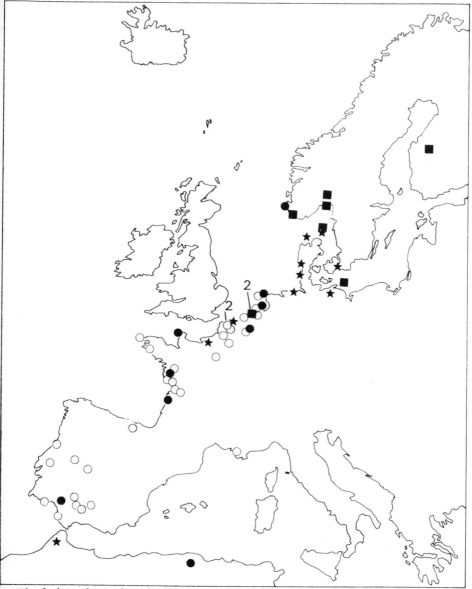

The finding places abroad of birds ringed in Britain during the autumn (NB those which were definitely youngsters when ringed are on the previous map). The season of recovery is shown by the symbol:

    Star – spring   Square – summer
    Black dot – autumn   Circle – winter.

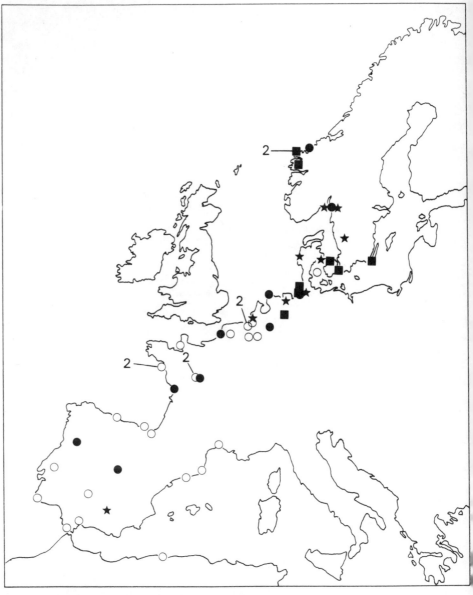

The finding places, abroad, of Robins ringed in Britain between January and April. The season of recovery is shown by the symbol:

Star – spring   Square – summer
Black dot – autumn   Circle – winter.

Recoveries of Finnish-ringed Robins during November to February; each dot represents the finding place of a Robin ringed during September and each star a Robin ringed in October.

become shy during their moult. How can birds that are present throughout the year undergo a migration?

The answer is that in Britain most individuals do not migrate at all. Detailed studies have shown that many birds take up a territory within a few hundred metres of the nest where they were hatched and remain in the same place, with just minor shifts of territorial boundary, until they die. It is also clear that there are two periods of dispersal when small shifts of location may occur — in the autumn when the winter territories are being set up, and in the winter and early spring when the breeding pairs are coming together. Even these short-distance changes could technically be called 'migrations' if they took place regularly each year for the same individuals; though that's stretching (or, rather, shrinking) a point somewhat. When we talk about 'migration' we really mean up-sticks and go; a proper movement to some other place.

With the Robin there is good evidence that males are most likely to remain in the same place and that it is the females that move house. The short-distance movements of British Robins are often to territories that are perfectly adequate for a single bird, outside the breeding season, but which lack suitable breeding sites for a nesting pair. For instance many newly built suburban housing estates have territorial Robins in the winter but breeding pairs are few and far between. In woodland areas there may also be a shortage of food during the winter and the abundant breeding birds (of both sexes) often move out to spend the winter in other habitats — for example reedbeds may provide excellent winter homes. A study of Robin territories on the little island of the Calf, off the southern tip of the Isle of Man, showed that over fifty Robins had winter homes on the island — very many more than had been bred there in the summer, showing that some of these winter residents were immigrants.

Still, although notionally similar, there is a big difference between a bird moving a few hundred metres from a woodland breeding territory to winter in a suburban garden and a bird travelling many hundreds of miles. It seems likely that about half of the British females move away from their summer areas for the winter. Most do not travel far but some do migrate overseas, as has been shown by ringing. Each record of a ringed bird which is found again and reported is called a 'recovery'. The first four maps (on pp. 21-4) show records of birds ringed in Britain and recovered abroad; the final one (p. 25) is of recoveries of Finnish-ringed birds. The first map has lines which join the ringing and recovery places. Some of the shorter movements shown may be long journeys for young birds, but there is a clear indication of a regular SSW migration in the majority of the records.

The longest distance moved by any of these birds was over 1,600km. This was a bird ringed as a nestling in Montgomeryshire in May 1966 which was reported as having been shot during the following January in the Spanish province of Badajos. The bird recovered in Switzerland was also ringed in 1966, as a juvenile in Surrey in July. Goodness knows what it was doing down there although, since it was found in April 1969, it had probably wintered further south — maybe in Italy. Only 18 birds are plotted on this map, a reflection of the fact that only a minority of British-bred Robins go abroad for the winter; if pressed, I would guess that it was less than 5% of females and probably hardly any males.

However, it has long been realized that large numbers of foreign Robins pass through Britain, particularly during the autumn but also in the spring, and that some birds from elsewhere may also winter with us. The first map only includes British birds ringed as nestlings or at breeding sites in May, June or July. The other three maps show recoveries of young birds ringed in Britain from August to the end of the year, older and unknown age birds from the same period and all birds ringed from January through to April (including a very few at migration sites in May). On all three maps those caught in summer (squares) are May to July, autumn (solid dots) August to November, winter (open circles) December to February and spring (stars) March and April.

All three of these maps show the same sort of movement oriented from the north-east during summer, into Fenno-Scandia, to the south-west during the winter into Iberia and North Africa. It is likely that a few birds of British origin are included but the summer reports from Belgium, Holland, Germany, Denmark, Norway, Sweden and Finland clearly show the main areas of origin. The final map of winter records of Robins ringed in Finland during September and October clearly puts the British records in context. Finnish birds spread much further to the east than ours do — there are even four recoveries in Turkey and a couple in Greece. However on the western side the recoveries look very similar to our own.

In Britain long-distance migration is an option taken by very few of the resident Robins. In areas like Finland it is imposed on all the native birds by the rigours of the winter. All along the northern limit of their breeding range Robins are long-distance migrants which leap-frog the intervening populations to winter along the southern edge of the species' breeding range. There is clear evidence, from the studies of migrating birds, that the males are much more likely to stay close to the breeding area than the females. It is obviously to the advantage of any male to get back onto the breeding territory and establish ownership before his rivals appear. But in difficult terrain, like the mountains of Switzerland, only about 10% of the breeding males are to be found wintering in the snow-free zones — the rest, and the females, leave for warmer areas.

If you want to see Robin migration in Britain, go to an East Coast Bird Observatory in the autumn. Robin migration takes place much later than the flight southwards of the bulk of warblers: in most years the peak is in early October. For instance in 1951 at the Spurn Bird Observatory on the northern edge of the Humber entrance, 152 Robins were caught on October 1st and another 394 were ringed by the 5th! Such numbers are exceptional, but, given the right weather conditions, 'falls' of hundreds of Robins may be recorded from several places along the coast on the same day: many species may be involved in such 'falls' but you have to be lucky to see one as the birds generally disperse very quickly indeed. Many of these birds have gone on to be recovered abroad and are figured in the maps. In southern Sweden, at the observatory at Falsterbö, the peak migration period is only slightly earlier than ours: around the last few days of September; in 1964 2,965 Robins were ringed. The later in the season the birds are ringed the further east they end up in winter; a fact explained by the later migration of populations from further east into Finland and Russia. Ringing work at Alpine passes has shown the peak passage there to be at roughly the same time as in Britain.

It is therefore clear that migrant Robins travel long distances very quickly. They do this at night (another reason why we don't normally notice them migrating). In fact they are classic medium-distance nocturnal migrants, just like Blackbirds and Redwings which reach us for the winter from the Continent. They do not travel as far as our summer visiting warblers and chats whose journeys are often 5 or 6,000km at a time. Robins are able to lay down a significant fat-store under their skin and in their body cavity, and use this as fuel on a long flight. Robins often weigh as little as 15g after migration and, had they started at 20g (a reasonable weight), the 5g of fat used as 'fuel' would have supplied enough energy for them to have flown continuously for 36 hours. At a speed of about 40kph this gives them a potential range of 1,400km of non-stop flight. A couple of flights would thus easily get a bird from the northernmost breeding area to the southernmost wintering grounds.

Some weight studies done on the Robins caught on Fair Isle (the tiny island between the Orkney and Shetland groups) indicate that this speed and level of weight gain is perfectly possible. Although not in any way an ideal habitat for Robins the birds that stayed on Fair Isle for at least five days, whether in spring or autumn, generally managed to put on 15% extra fat from an initial weight of 14.9g when first caught to 17.3g on recapture; the fat load is like a tank of petrol in a car, sufficient energy is stored on board for long distance travel – if necessary, without topping up. This is certainly enough to get them well south into England in the autumn or to take them safely across the North Sea into Scandinavia during the spring. Birds at this sort of weight would, as do all nocturnal migrants, take off in the evening as dusk closes in. The Fair Isle birds would probably then fly until first light and then come down for the day – unless they were still over the sea, in which case they would have to press on. The traces of birds (not necessarily Robins) doing just this have been seen on radar displays.

Of course we have so far begged the very obvious question of how Robins manage to navigate. This is very complicated and involves a much more precise ability than most people realize. Even the migrant Robins that winter 2,000km or more from their breeding place are quite likely to come back to the exact territory or very close by in order to breed the next year. They may even return to exactly the same winter territory in a subsequent year. Out of 101 ringed in winter in Gibraltar 5 were recaptured in later winters and of 37 caught and ringed overwintering in a nearby southern Spanish site 4 were found again a year later. The precision implied is tremendous, but we still do not properly understand how they do it.

Currently it is thought that the migrating birds use a wide variety of clues; for example, it has been proved that birds are able to use a 'sun-compass' to find the direction during the day. This means that, by watching the sun and its movement round the sky, they are able to work out, with good accuracy, the compass direction − N, S, E and W. In any case it is not much use to the Robin which is migrating by night! It has also been shown that birds can find their way using the position of the stars − in fact they learn where the pole star is (the point of rotation of the sky) and use that. If it is overcast at night they can use the earth's magnetic field.

This was discovered by a group of scientists working at Frankfurt. They first showed that birds kept in cages at night, without being able to see the sky or their surroundings, were able to orient themselves in the right direction for their migration. Then the research workers turned on a current in electrical coils

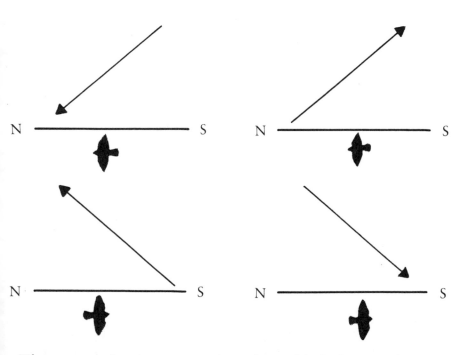

When we use a magnetic compass we know that north is the direction in which the needle points. The Robin does not use it like that but always treats the acute angle between the lines of force and the horizontal as north − clever birds, for the magnetic field reverses every half million years or so and will not, therefore, affect the Robins's ability to navigate.

fitted round the cage and the birds changed their orientation to fit the altered magnetic field. In fact it was discovered that the birds were using the acute angle made by the magnetic field as their goal and were not paying attention to the polarity of the field (see diagram). Recent research has shown that there is a minute speck of tissue in the bird's head with a concentration of magnetite (magnetic material) and this is where this sixth sense probably resides. The ability and the organ have also been found in humans — it is situated close to the nasal sinuses.

Birds can therefore use the sun, the stars and the earth's magnetic field to navigate. They may also use the long wavelength infrasounds produced by wind passing over mountains or waves on the shore (very low frequency and completely inaudible to us), the polarization of sunlight or even scents. In all probability species like the Robin have a whole range of navigation techniques at their disposal and use whatever is the most appropriate at any time. Whatever clues the birds are using to be able to point themselves in the right direction, it is this instinctive direction built into the birds' make-up that enables them to migrate long distances without being taught how to do it by their parents. Certainly the final part of their return journey will be undertaken using landmarks, for it seems inconceivable that the pinpoint accuracy of finding particular territory could be achieved with any of the other proposed systems.

Recognizing a landscape is obviously learned and not innate. The period when the young bird has just left the nest is probably vital both for learning landmarks and also for learning the star map. For the latter, experiments with the North American Indigo Bunting, reared indoors from the egg, have shown that it can achieve good orientation if it is exposed to a picture of the night-sky in a planetarium. But it only works if the sky is being rotated as it does in nature; if the display is static there is no sign of proper orientation. Even nonsense star maps, if properly rotated, enable the birds to orient themselves correctly. In fact the actual Pole Star is only north for a short period during a 22,000 year cycle; by each learning the actual star-map tens of thousands of generations of migrant birds have been able to travel accurately. We cannot tell what visual landmarks Robins use down on the ground; homing pigeons in towns use the shape and layout of buildings; Robins may use the shape of the landscape, prominent hills, large rivers, even roads and railways that look so conspicuous from even a few hundreds of metres up in the air. After all, early aviation pioneers managed long flights guided by such things, in the days before radio beacons, radar and other fancy navigational aids.

The timing of the spring migration is crucial. In Britain migrant females that arrive very late may find that all the best males are already mated. In the northern areas the earliest males to return will probably have the pick of the territories and the earliest females the pick of the males. Of course, there are risks: an early bird's arrival may also coincide with appalling weather conditions and, at best, it may survive in a weak state, at worst die. It is therefore a difficult decision for a Robin, when to time its spring flight. In general springs are becoming later over the whole of north-western Europe and recent research has shown that the arrival date of Robins in the region of Uppsala, in southern Sweden, is now nine days later than it used to be less than half-a-century ago. For the period 1941-50 the average date of arrival was April 3rd; by 1965-79 it had become April 12th.

How do Robins in Britain manage to maintain these two different strategies – mostly sedentary but a few migrating? Clearly there must be a balance of some sort within the population and advantages for each strategy. One of the clues lies in sex. Male Robins are a little larger than females and are therefore better fitted to survive in cold weather – indeed they may be able to win better winter territories than the females. The male also generally keeps his territory as part of the pair's breeding area and so winter territory is much more important for him than her. If she can afford to move a long distance to somewhere that provides easier winter conditions, she may have an advantage when she returns – particularly if the winter weather in Britain is bad and a disproportionately high percentage of the sedentary females perish. Computer simulations of similar situations have shown that only a slight advantage of migration, operating just once every few years, is sufficient to keep the migration option alive within a population – a sort of universal subconscious for Robins. Add to this the possibility of some migrant birds (probably more likely to be females) from the Continent staying to breed and pass on their habits and the process by which the two strategies might survive together can be understood.

The (erroneous) theory of transmutation

Before people understood that certain birds migrate at specific times of year, they were puzzled by the fact that apparently different birds lived in the same place at different times. Aristotle, who observed the changing bird populations in Greece, is supposed to have proposed a theory of 'transmutation': a change of form. He saw Redstarts in the Greek countryside during the summer but Robins in the same places during the winter. The numbers of birds involved were similar and the change happened again in reverse during the spring. The birds were similar in shape and habit and were the same size but different in colouring. These facts are reported in his writings and all the early translations ascribe to Aristotle the theory of transmutation: that the Redstarts turned into Robins and vice versa. It is a curious enough theory to us, but even more so because Aristotle did realize that migration took place with birds like storks, cranes and the large raptors. The flocks of such birds could be seen flying southwards in the autumn and returning northwards in spring. However, the little birds in the trees and bushes seemed to change without any mass movements of birds being detected travelling from place to place.

The theory of transmutation is repeated in dozens of books published during the Middle Ages and through to the eighteenth century. It was also suggested for other pairs of similar species: for instance, the Garden Warblers in Greece during the summer are replaced by wintering Blackcaps.

We now know that there is no truth whatever in the theory and that the real explanation lies in the large-scale movements of whole populations of birds. It was disproved by some early bird-keepers who caged Redstarts and Garden Warblers and found that they remained true to their species when they were kept over the winter. Recent scrutiny of the oldest available texts of Aristotle, in the original Greek, show that it is quite likely that he did not really believe in transmutation himself but was recording the facts as observed. Imperfect translation from the classics may therefore have given rise to a completely wrong and misleading explanation of the changes in bird populations during the year and have misled many generations of naturalists. Of course the natural transformation of the spotty juvenile plumage of the young Robin into its adult plumage, over a few short weeks in the autumn, is almost as wonderful as that which was erroneously ascribed to the birds a few centuries ago.

Weight

The average weight of a resident Robin in Britain is in the region of 19.5g (about 3 10p pieces; a pair of Robins weighs a bit less than a standard EEC size 4 chicken egg). Many ringers weigh the birds that they handle and so quite a lot is known about weight variations through the year and also about the growth in weight of the young birds. Since most people are unable to tell the sex of a Robin that they see, the figures quoted are not separated by sex. However, detailed studies, where individuals have been accurately sexed, show that the male Robins are generally a little heavier than the females. They also have slightly longer wings. Breeding females, in the process of laying eggs, have an inflated weight because of the eggs. Both sexes during the breeding season undergo development of their reproductive systems which increases their weights. In the males the testes and in the female the ovary (only one generally active) and the oviduct are enlarged.

When the egg is laid it weighs about 2.7g and gradually loses weight as the embryo develops. The loss is by transpiration through the shell and is the reason why well incubated eggs float. By the time it hatches, the egg has dropped to about 2.4g and the chick that emerges averages about 1.7g. It will grow steadily to reach almost 18g after ten days and then the weight increase slows right

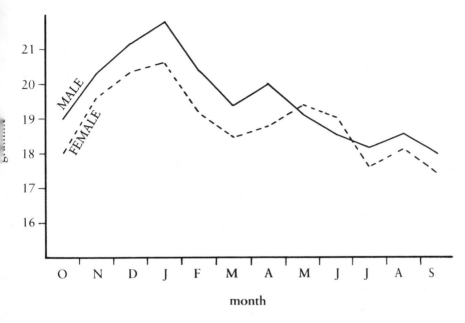

The annual fluctuations in weight of Scottish Robins shows a winter peak.
There is also an increase in weight of the females during the breeding season.

lown. At between 12 and 14 days of age it will fledge, all being well, at about
18.5g. These figures deserve a little thought. The breeding females often lay a
otal of six eggs in a clutch – the full weight of which represents about
90% of the adult bird's total body weight. By comparison a human mother
gives birth to only 10-15% of her body weight. The young, when they fledge,
are almost the same weight as the adults; so each parent will have had to find
the food needed for its own nourishment and also to produce a further 50g of
bird in the space of a fortnight.

Juvenile Robins out of the nest soon stabilize at about the same weight as the
adult birds. The annual cycle of weight variation follows that of many other
resident species. The peak weight, average over 21g, is during the mid-winter
months of December and January. The minimum average weight occurs during
July, August and September when it may be down to about 18g. This slimmed-
down trim figure is due to the fact that food is plentiful at this time of year and
the short nights are warm so there is no need for the birds to carry substantial
reserves to keep themselves warm or to tide them over periods of food shortage.

Migrant populations of Robins will also increase in weight in September and
October and again in March and April as they put on fat for fuel. Records at

bird observatories in Britain and abroad show that newly arrived migrating Robins regularly drop in weight to 15g or less and seem well able to survive. However, the few live birds caught weighing as little as 13g are almost certainly in grave difficulties. At some Scandinavian sites migrants return in the spring with weights of 19g or more. These birds have clearly been able to husband their resources well and will be able to survive and defend territories even if the weather is poor immediately they return.

The summer variations between roosting and waking weights may be as little as half a gram − and this is when the Robin's weight is at its lowest, this amount of fuel being enough to keep the bird going overnight. During mid-winter there may be more than 2g difference between the bird's weight during the day and when it is asleep at night: over the long cold night the bird must use up fat to provide warmth as well as keeping its body going. At this time of year there are only some eight hours of daylight and thus the birds must be able to gain weight at about 0.25g per hour if they are not to use up some of their reserves.

How many Robins in Britain?

It is very difficult to estimate the population, nationwide, of any common species of bird. The difficulty is compounded by the lack of attention given to our common birds by many birdwatchers − people always seem to be more interested in the rarities. Clearly the Robin is one of the commoner birds in Britain and Ireland. When the British Trust for Ornithology Breeding Bird Atlas Survey was finished, the Robin came out number eleven in the top twenty given below:

The twenty most widely distributed species from
The Atlas of Breeding Birds in Britain and Ireland:

Species	Total*	%	Population**
Skylark	3,775	98	2-4,000,000
Crow	3,767	98	1,000,000
Wren	3,755	97	10,000,000
Blackbird	3,718	96	7,000,000
Starling	3,707	96	4-7,000,000
Song Thrush	3,659	95	3,500,000
Pied Wagtail	3,646	94	500,000
House Sparrow	3,643	94	4-7,000,000
Meadow Pipit	3,642	94	3,000,000
Swallow	3,592	93	500,000+

ROBIN	3,591	93	5,000,000
Dunnock	3,574	93	5,000,000
Chaffinch	3,553	92	7,000,000
Mallard	3,549	92	150,000
Kestrel	3,546	92	100,000
Willow Warbler	3,536	92	3,000,000
Woodpigeon	3,536	92	3-5,000,000
Cuckoo	3,532	91	18-35,000
Blue Tit	3,473	90	5,000,000
Reed Bunting	3,431	89	600,000

* Total is number of 10km squares from which the species was recorded, out of the 3,862 such squares in Britain that were covered in the survey. The percentage refers to the percentage of squares where the species was found.
** Population estimates are breeding pairs in early 1970s.

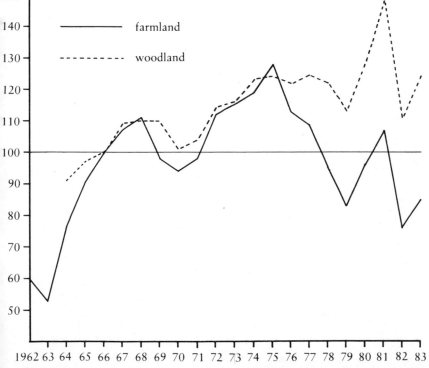

The British Trust for Ornithology has produced population indices for Robins for more than 20 years. The solid line is for farmland Robins and the dotted one for woodland ones.

The Robin map from the Atlas of Breeding Birds in Britain and Ireland: *by permission of the BTO and T and AD Poyser.*

These population estimates therefore put the Robin, with about 10 million birds, sixth equal among all British and Irish breeding species. All the estimates were constructed from known densities on breeding census plots and some very approximate calculations based on the areas of the different habitats available in Britain. A more recent estimate, using the same techniques, has provided a revised figure for Robins of about 3,500,000 pairs (i.e. 7 million birds). As we shall see, the 30% discrepancy may have been less to do with errors in the estimates than with fluctuations within the bird's populations. The densities of breeding Robins were at their highest in woodland: almost 70 pairs per 100ha (28 per 100 acres) when averaged for all types. The farmland average density is in the region of 13 pairs per 100ha and only about 2 in rough grazing land.

The maximum densities recorded were between 250 and 300 pairs per 100 ha in good deciduous woodland areas in lowland Britain (and even some parts of Ireland); with similar densities in large planted gardens. Robins were particularly common in sites like the Botanic Garden at Cambridge, where David Harper undertook his recent detailed study. In such areas Robins are often amongst the most common of breeding birds − for instance they made up 10.75% of the total breeding population of the Great Yew Wood at Kingley Vale, in Sussex, being just outnumbered by Chaffinches at 11%. Even in the very centre of London some 50 pairs breed most years but often nest sites are difficult for them to find in modern cities.

We know a good deal about the fluctuation of British Robin populations from year to year. For the last 20 or more years there has been an annual index of populations produced by amateur birdwatchers working together under the strict rules of the Common Birds Census (CBC) of the British Trust for Ornithology. For this the birdwatchers map the territories of all the birds breeding on their study areas and the index of population levels is produced by comparing the results from the same patch, surveyed by the same person, from one year to the next. In general the results for farmland plots show fluctuations of about 20% above and below an average level − hence a possible explanation for the difference in the two estimates of population given earlier. Both figures could be correct, but in different years. The levels at the moment are a little on the low side; at the end of the atlas fieldwork in 1972 they were at an all-time high.

Further population figures, from a Surrey oakwood, go back to 1946 and show similar levels of change as the more modern, national figures. In fact there are two indices calculated nationally: the one for woodland plots shows less variation than that for farmland. Generally, this is thought to mean that Robins are more at home in woodland and more at risk in farmland. In general all the lowest figures follow cold winters − notably 1947 and 1963 − but the population recovers very quickly. At its worst the Surrey wood held 19 singing Robins (1947) and at its best (1953) 33. The CBC index was at its worst on farmland in 1963 (53% of the 1966 level) and at its highest in 1975 (nearly a third higher than in 1966). The woodland CBC was not in existence until 1964 so that the full effect of the 1963 cold weather cannot be seen.

Local pressures on populations can often be seen at work. For instance at one of my ringing sites near Tring, in scrubland on a hilltop, the population was cut right back by the cold and snowy weather of the 1982 winter. My spring and summer catch was only about 10% of what I normally find. Only a few kilometres away, the population in Tring, where the birds had been fed in sheltered gardens all the winter, hardly seemed to have suffered at all. By the end of the 1983 season, with the young produced over two breeding seasons, I was again catching as many as ever − even on the hilltop site. Clearly Robin populations in Britain are very resilient and capable of bouncing back from anything that the British weather can throw at them. They do not show such wide fluctuations as species like Wrens and Kingfishers which may be very hard hit by freezing winters. In general, fluctuations in bird populations are 3-, 4- or 5-fold compared with 30-, 40- or 50-fold in some insect populations − remember the huge swarms of ladybirds and greenflies we had in recent summers.

How long does a Robin live?

Many people find it very difficult to believe just how short the average lifespan of a small bird like a Robin is. The oldest Robin, from more than 5,000 birds caught and reported to the British ringing scheme, had only lived for eight years and five months. A little thought will show why old age in Robins and similar birds is unlikely.

Taking a few simple figures for the productivity of breeding Robins and the undoubted fact that Robin populations in Britain are reasonably stable, it is possible to produce the following hypothetical figures:

1. Suppose that a population of 100 breeding Robins at the start of the breeding season forms into 50 pairs. Of these 45 are successful in raising

There are few, if any, Father Williams in wild Robin populations.

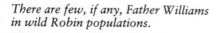

some young – let us say an average of 3 on each of two attempts for each pair. This means that the 100 adults have reared 270 young.

2. However, the population is not rising from year to year, so the 100 adults and 270 young must be reduced to 100 birds at the start of the next breeding season. (So 270 out of 370 must go. That's 73% who must die before next year.)

3. David Lack's annual survival rates, calculated from ringing recoveries, were 38% for adults and 28% for juveniles. This would give 38 adults and about 75 first year birds surviving to the start of the next breeding season – 113, which is a reasonable result, since we know that there are a number of territory-holding males that do not pair each year. These therefore do not figure in the productivity equations and would account for the figure being over 100.

This shows that Robins have a very difficult pattern of survival from man. With us, in the developed countries at least, there is little infant mortality and the majority of the population currently lives to approach the maximum lifespan. Indeed the proportion of old people in our population is steadily increasing. With the Robins there is huge infant mortality – as eggs, young in the nest and as recently fledged juveniles. All sorts of dangers affect even experienced birds and only just over a quarter reach one year, let alone 'old age' which, for a Robin, is probably ten or more years.

How does it die?

We will see elsewhere in this book that Robins may murder each other, be killed by cats, birds of prey, disease, etc. However it is very difficult to work out the importance of the different causes of death. Although these are the dramatic and obvious things that terminate a Robin's life, the real problem is probably shortage of food, for even a slightly weakened bird is at a grave disadvantage.

One way of trying to find out is to look at the causes of death reported by those who find dead ringed birds. Unfortunately the data is inevitably biased since birds which die as a result of disease or starvation, for example, are much less likely to be found and reported than those killed by cats or hit by cars.

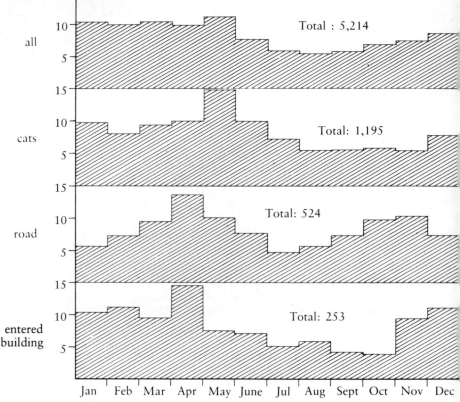

Percentage of ringing recoveries reported each month: for all recoveries (top) and for the three most commonly reported methods.

Anyone can diagnose what caused a Robin to end up squashed on the road and few people presented with a mangled Robin by a guilty-looking cat would assume something else had killed it. But how many people are going to look at a dead bird and say, 'Ah! coccidiosis' or 'nasty case of heavy metal poisoning'?

However the ringing 'recoveries' (ringed birds caught or found at a later date) do give some idea of the vulnerability of our Robins to different hazards over the year. The table shows eight specific causes reported, which accounted for more than 25 of the 5,216 recoveries; the runners up were: hitting wires (17) and being found on railways (14). Inevitably the majority of birds (2,199, or 42.2%) were simply reported as 'found' with no mention made of how they were found. Other categories like 'found injured' are hardly more helpful since the actual cause of the injury could have been a cat, a car, a hawk or a railway train.

Recovery causes of British-ringed Robins

Recovery cause	Total	Percentage
Cats	1,195	22.91
Killed on the road	524	10.05
Entered building	253	4.85
Traps set for another species	138	2.65
Owl or other bird of prey	86	1.65
In artificial water container	67	1.28
Cold weather	48	0.92
Hit glass	27	0.52

The impacts of cold weather and of predators are discussed elsewhere as are the risks of predation by cats and raptors. Birds that enter buildings may be seeking shelter or a nest site; often they can't find the way out and then starve. The unfortunate individuals that are shown as being caught in 'traps set for another species' are mostly killed in mouse-traps. Few people realize just how inquisitive Robins are when foraging and, just like mice and for the same reasons, they love cheese. The best way to avoid such mishaps is to put traps in dark places where Robins don't go. The birds found in 'artificial water containers' were mostly drowned trying to drink in water butts or cattle drinking troughs. These often have very steep sides and nowhere for the birds to perch. Hitting glass is a minor category for Robin mortality, accounting for only a tenth of the deaths so caused among some garden finches.

One way to look at the different pressures on Robin populations throughout the year in Britain is to express the percentage of all recoveries from each cause

in each month: direct comparison can then be made to see if there are seasonal changes. There are only enough recoveries of birds taken by cats, found on roads and entering buildings for worthwhile comparisons.

Clearly cat predation is particularly important whilst the parents are feeding their young during the breeding season. Road deaths are highest in April, as are recoveries indoors, these may both reflect the activities of birds which are searching for nest sites. Road deaths are also high in October and November but low during the two mid-winter months. Recoveries indoors are particularly frequent in November and December.

Skull nest

One amazing nest-site, recorded in a more barbarous age, comes from Trafford Green, near Chester. Two criminals were hung, for mail robbery, and their bodies left to hang in chains from 1796 to 1820. When they were taken down a Robin's nest was found in the skull of James Price.

Oh! James Price deserved his fate:
Naught but robbing in his pate
Whilst alive, and now he's dead
Has still robin in his head.

High he swings for robbing the mail,
But his brain of robin female
Still is quite full; though out of breath
The passion e'en survives his death.

The Robin's enemies

Robins living in the wild are subject to attacks by other animals just as they, themselves, eat insects, spiders and other invertebrates. Over the years there have been thousands of records of the remains of Robins that have been killed — by most species of owl and bird of prey as well as many small mammals. It is, however, the domestic cat which subjects British Robins to their most conspicuous attacks. This is because cats so often bring their prey indoors or leave the remains outside the back door.

In the previous chapter we saw that the overall proportion of mortality from cats was 22.9%, in fact very slightly more young than old birds reported. It has been said that cats do not like the taste of Robins but this does not seem to deter them. In any case many well fed cats will kill birds without needing to eat them; they also catch shrews — which certainly are very unpalatable. It is difficult even to hazard a guess as to the proportion of overall mortality for which cats are responsible. Almost any other cause of death will be under-recorded. However I would guess that cats cause between 5% and 10% of all Robin deaths in suburban areas.

The only other significant predators amongst the ringing records are 'owl or raptor' which account for almost a hundred recoveries (1.6%). These include birds whose rings have been found in pellets under the roosts of Kestrels, Tawny Owls, Barn Owls and Long-eared Owls and also bird remains found at Sparrowhawks' nests or their plucking posts. However these are much less likely to be found than rings from birds taken by cats. A Robin will probably be taken by most hawks, falcons or owls that happen upon it, but its worst enemy is undoubtedly the Sparrowhawk. Hunting Sparrowhawks generally watch for suitable prey from a perch in woodland and then dash at them over a short distance. In several studies Robins have made up more than 5% of all recorded Sparrowhawk kills. The Robin may also be killed by shrikes but in Britain the danger from summering Red-backed Shrikes is now minimal, for the population is here only in the summer and anyway is almost extinct; here now the Great Grey Shrike might take a few, but this too is a rare bird in Britain and only spends a few weeks here in the winter.

Increasingly, as the Sparrowhawk populations in south-east England recover, this is the fate of garden Robins.

However, serious bird predators not only take free flying birds — there are many species that will readily eat eggs or young in the nest. The worst culprits are undoubtedly the corvids: Jays in woodland and Crows and Magpies in more open country. All sorts of birds that one does not normally associate with nest predation would readily take advantage of the meal a Robin's or other small bird's nest would present. For instance, a Heron, Bittern, Water Rail or even a Moorhen would certainly take the contents of a Robin's nest, given a chance.

Small mammals attack nests too. Rats, stoats, weasels, hedgehogs, squirrels and mice commonly predate nests, as do foxes and badgers. Cats will play havoc with nests and their contents. Even dogs and, especially, escaped ferrets and mink, will devastate any nests they find. Snakes are not very numerous in Britain, but they also commonly feed on the eggs and young birds.

Robin parasites

Parasites are creatures most of us would rather not know about — being a parasite is a thoroughly underhand lifestyle and the parasites themselves have few redeeming features, being a motley crew of creepy-crawlies, worms and whatnot. That they should impose on our friend the Robin is an additional outrage, but the fact is that Robins harbour a very wide variety of parasites. However the birds do not normally suffer greatly, if at all, from their burden of

worms, fleas, lice, and other passengers. But if a bird is in poor condition, through another cause, then the deleterious effect of parasites may increase disastrously. An example is the problem experienced by a bird with a broken bill, which cannot then preen itself properly. In these circumstances the external parasites, like the feather-lice and louse-flies, may increase to such an extent that the bird begins to suffer.

External parasites are of four main types, three that feed mainly on blood and the fourth on feather material. The latter are the feather-lice (*Mallophaga*), which are tiny creatures spending their whole lives on the bird among its feathers. They chew the fine feather material for food and lay their eggs along the grooves formed by the feather plumes — securely sticking them on. The blood-sucking types include ticks, fleas and louse-flies (*Hippobscidae*). The ticks are picked up by many species that feed on the ground and often congregate in the

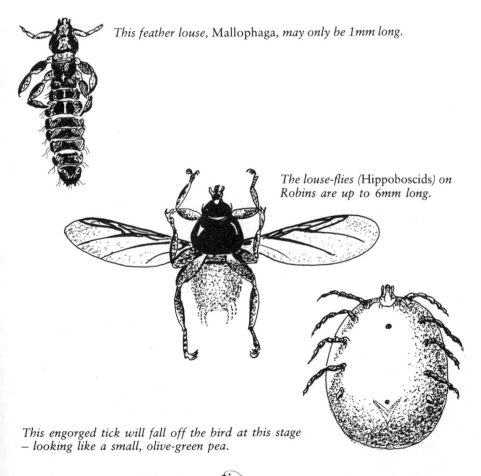

This feather louse, Mallophaga, *may only be 1mm long.*

*The louse-flies (*Hippoboscids*) on Robins are up to 6mm long.*

This engorged tick will fall off the bird at this stage — looking like a small, olive-green pea.

bird's ear; they drop off after feeding. The biggest ones are about the size of a small pea when fully engorged. Fleas are seldom found on Robins and have usually just hitched a lift for a mobile 'bed and breakfast'. This is because fleas produce larvae that live in nest linings (of birds as well as mammals). These develop for a while, often overwinter, then turn into an adult and invade a new host and feed on its blood. Thus specific fleas have developed on birds like Swallows, martins, etc., which regularly use the same nest, year after year, but not on species like Robins that do not return to last year's nest.

The louse-flies are some of the most interesting parasites. They are members of the same group as our common housefly but have developed very flat bodies so that they can scurry about within the stacked feathers of a bird's plumage. Louse-flies have hooks on their legs to help them hang on tight: an important consideration when their home and host may at any moment take to the air and fly fast, perhaps for several hours. Most species of louse fly have wings of their own so they can fly too, just in case of emergencies and also as an aid to swopping hosts. They are most often seen on birds in the summer and early autumn and are a constant hazard to we bird ringers with beards – a short flight and they have changed host! They are quite large – 6mm long – and often show a greenish tinge. They look very crab-like as they scuttle about among the plumage and Miriam Rothschild has described a small bird with a couple of them on it as being like a man with a couple of large shore crabs in his underclothes!

The commonest species of louse-fly on small birds in Britain is *Ornithomyia avicularia*. These creatures live most of their lives on the bird and give birth to tiny young, which later pupate and fall of the bird. The following year they have to find they way onto their eventual host when they emerge as adults in the spring: goodness knows how they manage!

In addition there are all sorts of internal parasites which affect birds, including Robins. Many of these are worms of various sorts which may be found in the gut – either absorbing food direct or feeding on the bird's blood. Other worms may attack specific organs in the bird – heart, lungs, windpipe or liver, or even exist in the bloodstream. A wide range of species have been recorded in Robins and related birds but their study is a very specialist subject and a great deal remains to be found out about them; not least how they get from the inside of one bird to the inside of another.

Disease

Disease probably takes a regular toll of all wild bird populations but it is very difficult to prove exactly what is happening. Individual birds that crawl off into dense cover and are unlikely to be found or, if discovered, subjected to an autopsy to determine cause of death. It is generally only massive deaths of birds

*This Robin has a fungal infection around its eye.
These may sometimes spread over much of the
bird's head.*

that are drawn to the attention of scientists and none of these plagues or
disasters, as far as I know, has especially affected Robins. In gardens the most
common disease outbreaks are of food poisoning (caused by *Salmonella*
bacteria) though this mostly affects Greenfinch flocks. This is a type of illness
that also affects humans, and is transmitted through infected droppings.

Robins are certainly affected by malarial diseases caused by the blood
parasite, *Plasmodium*, and other protozoans (single-celled animals) have been
found in their blood stream (like *Haemoproteus*), but it is not known what
symptoms these produce in birds. They are probably not a serious threat
normally as many birds survive with low rates of infestation in their blood.
Transmission of these organisms is probably through the bite of insects, ticks or
louse-flies. Other diseases caused by bacteria and viruses almost certainly affect
Robins but many types seem only to infect particular species of birds and almost
all the research has been done on more economically important species –
particularly poultry.

One disease that is known to affect Robins, and is quite often recorded from
garden birds, is 'alopecia' – the loss of feathers. In most cases this takes the
form of a fungal infection and is most apparent round the head. Sometimes you
may see an almost completely bald Robin. Analysis of the yellow encrustation
which accompanies this baldness has shown that it is made up of keratinized
skin with large numbers of fungal hyphae. In at least one instance the infection
has been specifically identified as 'favus' – a complaint that often affects poultry
and is caused by a skin fungus called *Trichophyton gallinae*. Some of these birds
have gradually recovered but others have disappeared and are presumed to have
died from their affliction.

Disease must, nowadays, also include pollution by man. Robins are not often
affected directly by agricultural chemicals, or those used in the garden, but it is
always possible for any bird that feeds on animal or insect material to ingest
disabled insects. These may include a sub-lethal load of poison which may, after
consumption of many tainted insects, build up in the bird's body. It is most
likely to affect birds at the top of the food-chain – like hawks and falcons – but
is also likely to be a hazard to Robins. Apart from cases of deliberate misuse of

chemicals, the most dangerous area for Robins has probably been in orchards where very powerful chemicals were used in the past. The best advice to gardeners must always be to use chemicals sparingly and only as directed on the packet/label. Putting in 'a little bit extra just to make sure' could be the downfall of many a garden bird, to say nothing of hedgehogs and even pets. It's all too easy to use chemicals to kill pests and forget that other links in the food chain might cop it too.

It is also likely that a few Robins die each year through asphyxiation when they nest in garages and are overcome by exhaust fumes — birds are very sensitive to carbon monoxide poisoning. It was for this reason that canaries were used in mines and it also explains the deaths of Starlings which may pass out and fall down a chimney when a fire is lit.

The Robin's year

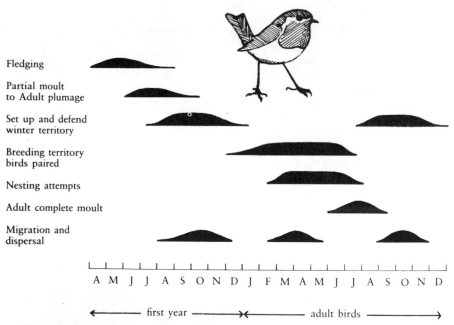

Fledging

Partial moult to Adult plumage

Set up and defend winter territory

Breeding territory birds paired

Nesting attempts

Adult complete moult

Migration and dispersal

A M J J A S O N D J F M A M J J A S O N D

← first year → ← adult birds →

The Robin's year is marked by some important activities which are undertaken, at about the same time, by the whole population. On this chart the bottom line (migration and dispersal) may not be important for the sedentary birds that only have a few metres to move.

The activities of an average British Robin, through the year, are given on the chart. The spring and autumn migration periods (shown on the lowest line) only affect a very few of the British birds (mostly females). This is the time of year when the birds from Europe pass through Britain and when British birds are most likely to disperse.

The majority of Robins are, of course, territorial throughout the year – except for the short period in the late summer or early autumn when they are moulting. The chart covers a period of 20 months to show what the young birds do, from the time they fledge, through a complete adult cycle. There are, of course, individual variations in timing as well as regional ones with, for example, a later start to the breeding season in northern areas than in the south.

The Robin's senses

We are so used to the way we perceive the world ourselves that we seldom stop to think how other creatures see, hear, smell and taste their surroundings. Even when, through experiments and observation, it is possible to find out their levels of discrimination, it is still difficult to imagine what it would be like to be another species.

It is certain that Robins, like all birds, are able to see in colour, and that their visual acuity – the sharpness of their sight – is as good as, and probably very much better, than man's. They have very much bigger eyes in relation to their body size than we do and are provided with as tightly packed receptors in the retina. The optic nerve and the part of the brain dealing with sight are also very well developed. They are able to focus through a wider range – from infinity to the tip of their beak – than most people are capable of. The relatively large size of the Robin's eye, and the regular activity of Robins at dusk and dawn, indicates that they also have good vision in low light intensity.

But anyone who has looked at a Robin will realize that it is only able to use binocular vision when looking immediately to the front: the eyes are on the side of the head and not, like ours, in the front. The advantage of this position is that it can see very well to both sides, above, below and even, to a certain extent, behind. The bird's normal, slight, head movements are probably enough for it to maintain a 360° watch. Anyone who has watched Robins will also realize that they are very aware of movement but will ignore stationary objects – even patient birdwatchers!

The Robin's sense of hearing is very similar to ours although the lowest frequency we can hear is several octaves below the bird's – infrasound detection, if it exists, is probably not through the ears. But the Robin is able to distinguish changes in pitch over very short time periods – thus what to us seem swift jumbled notes in a Robin's song will be clearly heard as separate and distinct phrases by another Robin.

The position of the Robin's ear — always covered by feathers.

There is little evidence that touch, smell or taste play very important parts in the life of small songbirds like Robins. Taste buds are few, compared with ours and the olfactory lobe (which receives scent) is also comparatively small. The main tactile sense in birds is probably associated with the tongue. The feet have few nerve endings and the outer sheath of the beak is horny and dead. However anyone who has watched a dismal Robin, standing on one foot on a snowy branch, will be sure they can tell when it is cold!

Of course the Robin does possess a sixth sense — the ability to detect magnetic fields — which it is now known that we also have; although the students who were tested demonstrated that it does exist in us, they were unable to describe how they used it — we are far short of knowing what it feels like for a Robin!

Plumage and moult

Anyone who has been lucky enough to follow a Robin's nest through to fledgling will have realized that the charming spotty youngster that emerges in the spring or summer undergoes a complete transformation during the autumn. By the middle of October all Robins are superficially identical with the familiar red breast, forehead fringed with grey, and the rest of the upperparts a plain rich olive brown.

After a variable period in their spotty juvenile plumage, the young Robins start to acquire their red breasts through a body moult in the autumn.

The first plumage is the fine fluffy sooty-black down found on the newly hatched chick. In the next two weeks, before leaving the nest, the juvenile plumage is grown whilst the whole family of youngsters are being fed by their parents. If food is very slow in coming the feathers grown during the period of shortage may be low in pigment, giving rise to pale bars across the feathers. In fact the colour on the part of the feather grown during the day is sometimes darker than that grown at night. On the Robin this can sometimes be seen as alternating dark and light bars on tail feathers.

If a young Robin has had an interrupted food supply whilst its first feathers were growing, fault bars, where the feathers lack pigment, may develop.

When the time comes for the moult from juvenile to adult plumage, old feathers are shed and new ones grown from various centres on the body. These are the feather tracts and the fresh feathers gradually grow outwards from them. For instance the orange breast colour starts from the upper centre and spreads outwards and downwards. Moulting birds are not easy to see for they are unable to hold territories as they have yet to grow the all-important red badge. However careful watching in the bushes of a large garden may give glimpses of the transitional birds. This moult generally takes about eight weeks. Some birds complete their post-juvenile moult within a few weeks of fledgling but others may remain in their spotted plumage for two months or more.

Although the birds seem to show a complete change of plumage, they actually retain their main flight feathers – the large wing feathers (primaries and secondaries) and tail feathers – until their second autumn. Some of the main coverts (the feathers that protect the bases of the major ones) on the wing are also retained – always the primary coverts and some secondary coverts too. The *alula* (the bird's thumb feathers) are generally kept as well. The secondary (or greater) coverts that are retained often have much more obvious pale tips than those on adult birds and bird ringers are sometimes able to age Robins in the hand using this character – even after the moult.

In fact estimating the age of Robins after the moult is not easy, even for ringers. The pale spots on the tips of greater covert may help but the best criterion is the colour of the bird's palate – the inside of the upper mandible (upper part of the beak). This is mostly yellow in young birds and dark grey in older birds. In addition, in common with many other songbirds, the tips of the juvenile tail feathers are narrower and more pointed than those of the adults. At their tips the edges of the feathers also suffer very slight but characteristic damage during the time they are growing in the nest. This is permanent and can help to distinguish young birds for a few months in the autumn – but only in the hand, as these details often need to be studied with a hand-lens.

Finally ringers can also check to see if the two layers of bone on the top of the skull are fully developed. The newly fledged birds have but a single layer of bone on top of the skull, then gradually a second inner layer grows with an air space between. Over a period of three or four months these two layers are joined by columns of bone which strengthen them. Thus if the feathers are parted in the autumn a pale patch on the skull speckled with white dots indicates the fully ossified part of the skull but unossified areas coloured pinkish (without the white dots) are only found on young birds. It is not an easy technique to use but has been found to be a very useful check. Luckily the Robin's skin is usually fairly transparent – there are some irritating birds with dark skin in which the degree of skull ossification is invisible (through the skin).

Adult birds also undergo a complete moult (including the flight feathers) during the autumn. This is the only time of the year when adults are not fully territorial and it also punctuates the short, silent gap between the different seasonal songs. After the moult all will sing the more plaintive and wistful autumn/winter strains (see p. 93). The moult is very important as the feathers of the adults gradually wear out and become less efficient for both flight and insulation. The body feathers moult in much the same way as those of juveniles, but the flight feathers have to be moulted and re-grown in a controlled sequence which allows the birds to continue to fly with reasonable efficiency.

The wing feathers are the most vital. Their moult starts in the middle of the wing: the primaries moult outwards and the main secondaries moult inwards (see A). The very first flight feather to drop is invariably the innermost primary and each successive primary is shed at four- to five-day intervals (see B). When the fourth has dropped the middle tertial is lost (see C) and when the fifth primary has dropped (and the inner two are almost full grown) the outermost secondary is lost (see D); in this way the gap created by the moulting secondaries and primaries never joins. At the end of the moult the small outermost primary is fully grown when the ninth is still only a third size – at this stage (see E) the innermost secondary is still growing. Tail moult is from the centre pair outwards and spans most of the period when the primaries are moulting.

The duration of primary moult is about two months and just about covers the time taken for the renewal of the body feathers. Thereafter, moult generally starts annually at the end of the breeding season – which varies from bird to

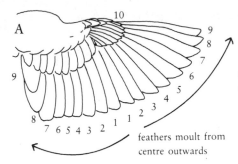

A

The extended right wing of a Robin before the moult has started. The outer main wing feathers – the primaries – are numbered outwards and the inner ones – secondaries and tertials – inwards.

feathers moult from centre outwards

The main moult has started with the two innermost primaries dropping in sequence and starting to regrow.

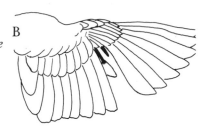

B

C

Now the innermost primary is fully grown and only 6 old primaries remain: at this stage the 8th secondary (or central tertial) is dropped.

Primary moult continues, the outermost secondary has dropped and another tertial is being renewed (secondary 7).

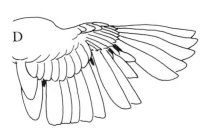

D

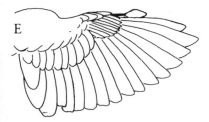

E

Wing moult almost complete with only the outermost primaries and the 6th secondary growing.

bird. In most years a number of Robins will have started to moult before the end of May but others, whose breeding season has been extended, may not have started to moult until the beginning of August.

The period of moult is a time when the birds are vulnerable, for their flight potential is impaired and they need to take in extra food so that they can grow the new feathers. They are also not defending territories and are at a very considerable disadvantage if they encounter unmoulted or fully renewed Robins which are defending territories. However the summer and early autumn is a time of plentiful food and it is unlikely that too many adult birds in the course of their complete moult suffer much stress. There are pros and cons for each timing: birds that have a late moult may have the advantage of holding territory and even having an extra breeding attempt in the late summer. On the other hand birds that start and finish early may be able to set up territories early and so appropriate really good sites for the coming winter.

There is another 'moult' which takes place at the beginning of the breeding season. This only affects the females and is the loss of feathers from the belly to form the brood patch. This is the area of bare skin which is kept warm by many blood vessels and provides efficient heat transfer between the adult bird's body and the eggs (or nestlings). The feathers lost from the brood patch are replaced during the normal annual moult which follows the breeding season, when the need for a heat radiating bald patch is passed. Even when they have a fully developed brood patch adult birds generally have rather more body feathers than the newly fledged youngsters.

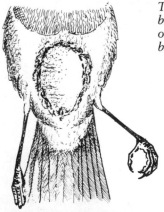

The bare brood patch, developed in the breeding season by female Robins, is only apparent in the hand when the belly is gently blown.

The juveniles will shortly undergo a complete body moult and so the plumage grown in the nest need not have the good insulation a bird would need for survival through the winter.

Territoriality

Most birds are territorial during the summer when they are breeding. The Robin is one of the few species in Britain that is territorial through almost all the year. During the spring and early summer the breeding territories are held jointly by the pair but, at most other times of the year, each male and each female Robin has to defend its own space. This territoriality of both sexes is the reason that both sexes sing and that Robin song is with us for almost the whole of the year, since song is one of the main ways of proclaiming a 'territory'.

Physical combat, like this, seldom lasts long before one bird backs down.

The fact of the Robin's territorial behaviour has been well known for a very long time — for example, 2,200 years ago Zenodotos wrote: *Unicum arbustum haud alit duos erithacos* ('A single bush cannot harbour two Robins'). The classic work on Robin territories was done many years ago by David Lack in England and by J.P. Burkitt working at Enniskillen in Northern Ireland. They both used colour rings, placed on wild birds, to identify individuals and were then able to plot exactly which areas were used by each bird.

The illustrations on the next page show the territories which David Lack found in the area of Dartington Hall, Devon, in the breeding season and at mid- October from April 1935 to April 1938. The territories cover orchards, woodland and quarries with a large building in the top right and some open fields which lacked birds. Most of the Robins were sexed by their behaviour during the breeding season and almost every one had been ringed so that its identity was known. Birds appearing on more than one map have a serial number to identify them — M6 appears on all but the first map and F3 on the last four

The first point to notice is the differences in size and shape of the territories. In fact they are liable to change throughout the year — both because of gradual adjustments of boundaries and sudden changes caused by the death of a bird or the arrival of a new one. In three of the four breeding seasons there were

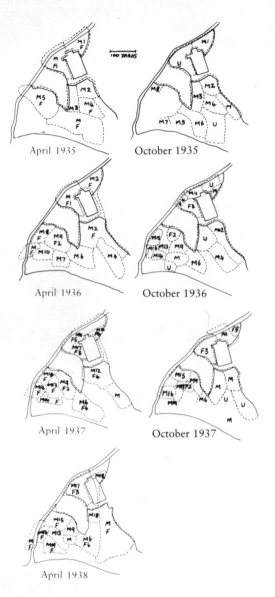

The territory maps shown here are from David Lack's classic study. The sex of the owner (owners) is shown by M – Male, F – Female or U – Unsexed. Any individual bird that appears on more than one map has also been given a number – for example, Male No. 1 appears on the first two maps, Female No. 3 on the last four. Those without numbers only appear on one map.

territories that spanned the large building – one (M18 in 1938) was a bachelor male but the other two were breeding pairs. The largest territories were owned by breeding pairs and averaged 0.55ha (1.36 acres) although some pairs had permanent territories only half this size and a few half as big again. Larger breeding season territories (up to 1.32ha or 3.26 acres) were not maintained for long. In years when populations were higher (for instance 1937 compared with 1935) territory sizes were rather smaller without apparently inconveniencing the birds: they were able to breed successfully. The unmated males, during April, held smaller territories than the mated pairs (average 0.35ha) – comparable with the average size of the October territory (average 0.30ha). The smallest winter territories were only 0.07ha (800 sq. yd). The lower numbers of females in the winter are explained in the chapter on migration.

The majority of the marked birds that stayed within the study area retained at least a part of their territory from season to season. A few went missing for a period – for instance the October 1937 maps show no records for M17 or F6 although both were present in the 1937 and 1938 breeding seasons. Both birds were paired to the same mates in each season (M17 with F3 and F6 with M6) and these mates had defended part of the pair's territory through the winter. In fact of 34 successive appearances on the maps by males only three fail to include a substantial part of the previous range: for ten successive appearances of females only one showed a shift.

What is the point, for the Robin, in staking out and defending a territory? So much time and effort goes into the activity that it must clearly have a real benefit for the birds involved. The two main theories have been, firstly, that it is essential for the male to have a territory for him to be able to attract a mate and, secondly, any Robin must have a territory in order to be able to secure a reliable food supply. David Lack's detailed observations, at first sight, scuppered both these ideas. He showed that females also defended territories during the winter – although there was a preponderance of males – and so it was not just

a question of the males trying to ensure a place for their mates. Also his detailed observations showed that the territory-holding bird, or birds, quite often feed outside their defended area and will tolerate other birds that want to feed within it. This is well known by ringers who sometimes catch as many as six or eight Robins within a small garden in one day during the winter — generally when food is being put out for the birds.

Current thinking about the problem centres on the behaviour of the organisms on which the Robin feeds. Unlike vegetable items — seeds or fruit — most of the Robin's food is itself alive. The invertebrates do not want to be eaten and so are likely to hide or 'freeze' if they realize that there is a Robin or any other bird predator about. This means that the Robin, which is a territory holder, can search a part of its own area for a short while and then move on. Since it will not be back for quite a time it will know that the spiders and other invertebrates that it missed the first time are quite likely to have forgotten it and have re-emerged on its next visit to that exact spot. The actual feeding behaviour of the Robin seems to be sufficiently distinct for it not to be worth the investment of time and effort, on the Robin's part, to try to defend its territory against any other species — or even a few feeding sallies by adjacent Robins. Some more recent observations have shown that when males and females from adjacent territories pair, each may still do almost all its feeding in those parts of the communal area which 'belonged' to it during the winter.

The main means of territorial defence, for the established bird, is its song. In most cases the territorial bird only has to sing at a potential rival for the intruding bird to give way. Individual recognition is promoted by the variability of the Robin's song and so adjacent established birds can hear and recognize the songs of their near neighbours. However, an interloper who is trying to establish a territory from scratch may face up to the owner and start to sing, rather quietly to start with, in its territory. Such provocation will cause the resident bird to fly directly at the newcomer who, if it persists, may be physically attacked. Such fights may be to the death (see Murder on page 61) but most often the intruder gives way. New territories are usually established by birds which manage to insinuate themselves into peripheral areas and may then gradually expand into the fringe parts of other birds' areas.

The threat posture of a male Robin to a rival on the same level involves much puffing out of the breast feathers to show the maximum amount of red plumage.

The other territorial defence is for the birds to display at each other but this generally happens between established neighbours — they get to know each other quite quickly — at the territory edges. Robins seldom attack other species within their territories although there are a few records of Dunnocks being harried by particular individual Robins — they may have been colour-blind or simply got out of the nest on the wrong side that morning.

Display and aggression — murder

Most species of birds and other animals have evolved elaborate means of avoiding conflicts between themselves that are likely to cause real damage. It is often argued that man's apparently insatiable appetite for fighting and war is *unnatural* and that wild animals do not show such tendencies. Examples of the behaviour patterns that stop Blackbirds from hurting each other can be seen every spring on almost any garden lawn. The male Blackbirds, torn between wariness and bold assertiveness, parade up and down, separated by an invisible demarcation line which marks the territorial boundary between them. If either bird crosses it, the other is dominant and the intruding bird quickly returns to its home ground. On the bird-table a Greenfinch will flick its wings and turn on another Greenfinch that is too close and this one will give way — blows are seldom struck.

With the Robin the territory-owner fluffs out his or her red breast feathers and seeks to find a higher perch than his/her opponent. An intruder in the territory will respond to such posturing by submitting and retreating whilst the

Aggressive Greenfinch males are often top bird at the feeding station.

neighbouring bird, on the edge of the two territories, will also display to maintain its own position. Actual fights are therefore avoided in the day-to-day activities of the established birds. However this is not the end of the story, for the possession of a good territory is the Robin's key to survival.

During the winter, when the food resources available for Robins may be very low, only those birds that have been able to defend a territory containing sufficient reserves are able to survive. In the spring only the males with good territories will be able to attract mates and find sufficient food to breed successfully. If there is a great deal of food available the territory-holding bird may allow others to feed freely, particularly when the weather conditions are bad, but those birds 'allowed' in will always be rather nervous and will readily give way if the territory-owner wishes to assert his rights of possession. This is why several Robins can be seen feeding together at a garden feeding station in periods of very severe weather, despite their territoriality.

Most species of birds in Britain only hold territories during the breeding season but the Robin clings to its patch all year round and only relinquishes its personal territory for the short period when it undergoes a complete moult in the early autumn. At other times of the year the available ground, suitable for

Robins, is as precisely partitioned between the individual birds as the plots on the local allotment are between the gardeners. Any bird without its own territory is doomed to die and so it has a tremendous incentive to try to carve out a patch. Getting a territory becomes a matter of 'do' or 'die'. This is where murder may be committed in a quick, brutal and utterly clinical manner.

Most often the intruder will announce its presence by singing within the owner's patch. This will immediately provoke a bout of angry singing in reaction and aggressive posturing by the possessor of the territory. Now the intruder must make up its mind — it could still retreat and get away with no more than damaged pride. However, if it persists, the owner will fly straight to it and attack. The first flurry of blows may be enough to settle the matter and the loser (generally the intruder) may be able to get away from the winner. However if battle is really joined it is not unusual for there to be a dead Robin within a few minutes. Generally the winner will have pecked at the loser's head and even exposed the brain.

It used to be thought that this was an unusual circumstance brought about by peculiar local conditions. For instance Bruce Campbell watched a battle to the death in an enclosed courtyard where he thought that the loser was unable to get away because of the walls around it. However recent detailed observations have shown that this is not always the case and murder is rather more frequent — possibly accounting for over 10% of all deaths in some populations. It is the ultimate proof of the importance of territory for the Robin — the defeated birds die, but at least they have tried. Maybe the feuds between humans are not so unique after all.

In the past the murder victims were often thought to have been killed by cats or other predators. However it is very unlikely that such dead Robins, in otherwise good shape and only damaged around the head, have been killed by cats or raptors because if they had, the carcase would be more extensively damaged and even partially eaten. These deaths can occur at almost any time of the year but are less frequent during the breeding season when the breeding birds have to spend so much of their time feeding their offspring. Murder is probably most common in the early winter when winter territories are being set up and in the earliest parts of spring when the breeding territories are being demarcated.

It would be wrong for us to mortalize, using human value judgements; the birds have evolved a system of existence which ensures the continuance of the species and its occupation of almost all areas suitable for the species.

The territorial system which runs through almost the whole year *requires* that the fit and healthy birds should defend their territorial plots and so ensure that it they that are able to breed during the next breeding season. It would not be in the interests of the species as a whole for the inferior birds to survive at the expense of the fitter ones.

In most cases where a bird comes into a new area to carve out a territory it will try to insinuate itself into the mosaic of defended Robin patches. In many populations not all the area is covered by defended territories and some, admittedly poor quality, corners will be vacant. A really aggressive intruder will use this base to filch a few metres here, a few there. A self-effacing bird may try to stick out the winter on its own poor patch — successfully in mild years but often dying if the weather closes in.

In case this ferocious aspect of Robin behaviour seems so out of character that you do not believe it, there are some simple experiments which anyone with Robins in their garden can carry out, to prove it for themselves. The red on the Robin's breast is what provokes the attack from the defender of the territory. As a ringer who handles wild-caught Robins and possessing a red beard, I have had them display at me whilst I have been ringing them. It is easy to provide a stuffed Robin, a *papier mâché* model or even a brown Robin-sized and shaped bundle of rags at first without a red 'breast'. Put this in a bird's territory in late February or March and it will almost certainly be ignored: then paint on the red breast and you may see the resident bird tear it to pieces in the course of a few minutes of frenzied attack.

It would, of course, be very unfair to leave such a stimulus within the bird's territory for any length of time. The bird would waste a great deal of energy and time on pointless attacks and might not be defending the other parts of its territory from real intruders.

Reactions of nesting Robins to other species

During the breeding season most pairs of Robins do not bother about the presence of other species. However there are exceptions to this general rule — quite apart from Cuckoos coming to oust baby Robins and the Robin parents attempting to defend their brood from potential predators. When Robins do get involved with other species the relationships take a variety of forms — ranging from cohabitation to violent attacks.

There are a number of instances where Robins have used the disused nest of another bird as the base for their own. Several times old Blackbird or Song Thrush nests, generally within or beside buildings, have been used successfully as a nest-base by Robins. I have found Robins nesting in the partly collapsed burrow of a Sand Martin and there have been stories of Robins taking over old Swallow's nest sites. The most remarkable instance was found by Gordon Booth, near Otley in Yorkshire during 1967. A Robin and Redstart shared the same open-fronted nestbox — each laid 5 eggs but 3 of the Redstarts were removed by the observer as they were in danger of tumbling out (also, for small birds like Robins and Redstarts, 7 is really the maximum number of eggs they can successfully incubate). Both hens incubated, generally on their own, but sometimes side by side; once the Redstart was seen sitting on top of the incubating Robin! Most of the eggs hatched, but the nest was soon predated by a Magpie. Another Robin sat on a mixed clutch of Great Tit and Robin eggs and hatched the former — again the nest was raided early on and probably before the Robin's own eggs had been fully incubated.

Aggression during the breeding season between two species has seldom been recorded. However there is an instance of a Blue Tit smashing a clutch of Robin's eggs (but not eating them) some 30m from its own occupied nest. There is also a report from Merseyside in 1977 of a Robin eventually killing a brood of Song Thrush chicks some 15m from its nest. In its mitigation, these birds had been very badly behaved with regular fights between the Robins and the Song Thrushes.

Stories of aggressive interactions are actually outnumbered by reports of Robins helping other birds out by feeding young or fledglings of other species. Obviously the stimulus provided by a chick with a wide open gaping mouth is one that parent birds, especially Robins, find difficult to resist. In Britain Song Thrush, Blackbird, Spotted Flycatcher and Willow Warbler have all been reported as helped by Robins. In some cases such feeding was regular and happened both whilst the young were in the nest and continued after they had fledged.

In France, during 1977, a Robin regularly fed a brood of Long-tailed Tits. In this case the circumstances were a little odd as the same bush that held the tit's nest had held a Robin nest with 11 eggs a few days earlier. The Robin's nest, whose clutch was probably from two females, was deserted and it was supposed that the 'surplus' female helped with feeding the Long-tailed Tits as an outlet for her maternal instinct. Possibly the fact that most of these reports of adults feeding the 'wrong' chicks refer to adult Robins adopting other species indicate a strongly developed maternal instinct among Robins. It is unusual to hear of the boot being on the other foot (or claw) and a baby Robin being fed by something else, but one such story (also from France) tells of a baby Robin, out of the nest, being fed by an adult Wood Warbler.

Time to breed

For most British Robins the breeding season starts in March — unless the weather is very bad. The peak period for which newly completed clutches are recorded is mid-April and there is little doubt that most pairs try to rear two broods, many make three attempts and some even four. The final attempt is usually in June so that young are often in the nest until mid-July. Really late clutches may not be completed until the end of July.

Although this is the normal pattern, in fact there are records of Robins attempting to breed in Britain during every month of the year. February has been quite common in years with a very early spring and some of these attempts were successful. The single published record for September (Suffolk) was also successful. Another nest, this time in Dorset, fledged young at the end of November and a Norfolk pair successfully raised five chicks from a nest of young which hatched on December 8th. An Irish pair with fully fledged young on February 7th must have completed their clutch in the first half of January. However most breeding attempts at unusual times of the year are failures. Out of season breeding attempts probably fail directly through lack of food and also lack of time to gather it — due to the short day-length. However the birds may possibly have been conned into trying to breed at an unseasonal time of the year through the influence of artificial lights. These could upset their circannual rhythm, which governs the development of their reproductive system, controls the moult cycle, etc, through the bird's hormonal balance. If this is the case they may have opportunities for feeding during the hours of darkness. They may also have been brought into breeding condition through the lavish provision of food at a feeding station. They could still have a problem feeding the nestlings since the food provided is unlikely to be the varied mixture of naturally occurring invertebrates suitable for growing youngsters.

Within each breeding attempt the timing of the various activities is fairly standard. The female lays her eggs, one each day, usually in the early to mid-morning. One charming description of a nest in a bedroom describes the female as giving a quick burst of song immediately after she had laid the egg — was it relief or triumph? Incubation starts when the last egg is laid (or sometimes with the penultimate one and sometimes a day after the last) and is almost exclusively undertaken by the female. She spends much longer, during daylight, on the nest than off it and has a good deal of her food provided by the male away from the nest.

The eggs generally hatch after 13 days, although 14 is not unusual. Most reports of 15 days refer to early nests where the start of incubation may have been slightly delayed. The fledgling period, during which both parents feed the nestlings, averages about 14 days but 13 and 15 days are frequently recorded. Birds leaving the nest prematurely, on the 11th or 12th day, have probably been disturbed but may still survive. The young, out of the nest, are tended by their parents for up to three weeks. If another breeding attempt is being made the majority of the post-fledgling duties may be undertaken by the male whilst the female gets on with the next clutch. Some second nests may even be started before the young have fledged but most are not completed until the previous brood has been out of the nest for about ten days. If a breeding attempt fails the female will generally build a new nest and lay the first egg of the replacement clutch within a week.

After it has hatched the young Robin is completely dependent on its parents for food and warmth.

At four days the baby Robin needs to be in the protected environment of the nest but can already stand upright and beg for food.

Young Robins, like this one, which have just left the nest are often unable to fly properly for 24 to 36 hours.

Pairing up

Traditionally February 14th, St Valentine's Day, was thought to be the time when breeding birds, of many species, paired up. For the Robin this is certainly not the case and the actual date of pair formation varies from late December through to early March. Pairs which result in breeding attempts may even be formed as late as mid-May but these are generally late because a 'spare' female has become available; probably because tragedy had overtaken her mate. In most years there are surplus unmated males holding territories throughout the

breeding season. It may be that producing the eggs, incubating them and brooding the young are dangerous pursuits which lead to a higher mortality for the female than the male.

There is no conclusive evidence that Robins are able immediately to decide on the sex of an intruder into their territory. The male territorial Robin, singing loudly and persistently with his spring song, is undoubtedly recognized, as such, by a wandering female. He, however, seems not so perspicacious, and when she first enters his territory his initial reaction is generally aggressive − in defence of his rights − and it is only when the female fails to respond as an intruder would that the pair begins to come together. Generally the female flies up to the male who may sing and react aggressively before moving off − the female responds by following him. In this way she becomes accepted by the male over a period of a few hours − interspersed by bouts of feeding by both birds.

By the time the male starts to follow the female it is odds on that they will become a breeding pair but there are some records of 'broken engagements'. In most cases it is the female who transfers her affections to a neighbouring, unmated, male. The pair of birds generally enlarges its territory to cover a considerably bigger area than the single male was defending on his own. In some cases this is very easily done, for a territorial female may pair with her next door neighbour − a ready-made double-sized territory. In other cases the pair will encroach on their neighbours' areas: particularly space belonging to any unmated males. Often it will be the hen that first ventures over the boundary and new parts are annexed if she is not repulsed.

Since pair formation may have taken place two or three months before breeding activity starts it is surprising, to most people, that pairs are not seen together in the spring. In fact most of the time is spent feeding − a solitary activity − and so they seldom come together. Indeed there are records of severe weather causing the two birds of a pair to separate and defend half the breeding territory against the other! However, generally the two birds have become used to each other and can certainly recognize one another over a range of 25 or 30 metres.

When both birds of an established pair survive and are resident in an area during the winter their separate winter territories are often two halves (more or less) of the breeding territory. Undoubtedly these birds recognize each other and there are indications that even the winter territories may be shared — this is obviously not too easy to prove as the individual birds will each have their own favourite parts for feeding.

Detailed studies of Robin populations through the year in Britain have all shown that many of the female birds are missing during the winter. These are birds which have migrated — possibly only a short distance to take up territory in an area unsuitable for breeding birds, possibly overseas (p. 21). The return of these birds in the spring brings about the formation of further pairs — in just the same way that the residents get together — but, for some of these, there may be only a few days between pair formation and the start of breeding. In studies where marked migrant females have been seen to return in the subsequent breeding season there are several records of the same territory being occupied — but also some when it wasn't. In one case, in David Lack's Dartington Hall study, the female moved to a different territory even though her mate, of the previous year, was in possession of part of their former area.

Drunkenness

As the Christmas bird par excellence it seems appropriate to record the Robin which managed to imbibe too much of the Christmas spirit. Some fifty years ago Margaret Holden wrote of the household Robin which, having eaten its share of the plum pudding and brandy sauce, fell off the chair back on which it was resting. Left in a safe place to sleep off the effects, it never touched another drop!

Courtship feeding

Courtship feeding takes place between the cock and hen of established pairs. The female gives a begging call, very like that given by a hungry youngster, and the male gives her some food. In fact this is only part of the story because, throughout the period when courtship feeding takes place, the female is also giving juvenile-like contact calls to the male and it is almost certainly these that trigger the feeding behaviour. Although courtship feedings starts immediately after the nest has been completed, before any eggs have been laid, it happens with increasing frequency through the laying and incubation periods.

You would assume that the female benefited from being waited on, but some detailed studies by Marion East seemed at first sight to show that the female had little need of help, she was well able to feed herself and made an average of two attempts to catch prey for every minute spent foraging; whereas, even at its most frequent (during incubation) she only received a feed every five minutes from the male. However she was not always successful when feeding herself and the male invariably presented her with a bundle of food which would normally contain five or more items — as much as she could get herself in 150 seconds if she was being successful every time she tried to take prey. Thus the male was probably able to provide well over a third of his mate's food requirements during incubation.

Marion East found that the females who were most insistent with their contact calls were also fed more frequently by their mates. They produced larger clutches than females with lower contact call rates and were therefore likely to fledge more young. It has also been suggested that the female is able to judge, soon after completing the nest, whether the male she is with will be able to provide food for her and their brood efficiently. In other words if the male fails to live up to her expectations she could go off and find another. Unfortunately most detailed studies can only cover a small area and, if this does happen, the female would probably move too far to be detected after she had jilted her idle mate. However, in all the Robin populations so far studied, males are usually more numerous than females and so she is likely to be able to exercise such a choice.

Adult Robins exchanging food are always a breeding pair — male feeding female.

Family life

Generally Robin adults only pair for the duration of the breeding season. Undoubtedly, after the pair has been formed, the cock and hen know each other as individuals both by sight and through calls and song. After the pair has been formed, sometimes as early as December, the adults may seldom come together but, as the breeding season approaches, the female will start to consort with the male. In fact, in almost all cases which have been studied closely, it is the hen that selects the nest site and builds the nest. There are several records of the hen being observed to chase away the male if he approached whilst she was building. During this period courtship feeding starts and also copulation happens.

Sex between consenting Robins seems a rather casual happening. With little or no preliminaries the female invites the cock to mount by adopting a hunched posture with head lowered. The male jumps onto her back, and, with a twist of their tails, their cloacas meet. It is all over in a few seconds and may happen several times a day over about ten days — spanning the end of nest building and the completion of the clutch.

During incubation the male is aware of the position of the nest and may call to warn the female if danger approaches. The female is fed by him away from it and on demand. The hatched eggshells are discreetly removed and dropped some distance from the nest. It is the female who broods the tiny young and the male provides most of the early food. Both parents assiduously feed the young when they are a little older and participate in the chore of nest sanitation – the droppings formed by the nestlings are neatly wrapped in a mucous-like membrane and can be taken from the nest and dropped at a distance by the parents — sometimes they are eaten. Droppings over the edge of the nest would be both messy and conspicuous.

The female may often leave much of the care of the fledged young (which

The young Robin immediately after it has fledged is spotted, with no sign of any red on its breast.

mainly consists of feeding) to the male — anyway with early broods — so that she can get on with the next clutch. For the final brood the parental responsibilities for the fledged young are shared and the two adults may drift apart — or share the same area. When the adults begin their moult co-operation ends and often they will taken up territories some distance apart. However there are a number of pairs which have been known to set up adjacent territories and then to breed together in a later year; sometimes they may share winter territories.

Divorce

There are quite practical reasons to expect that paired Robins, who have successfully bred together, should remain paired for their second and subsequent broods and also in later years (if both survive). The fact of their first success should indicate that they will be able to do it again: thus each should be able to pass its genes on to the next generation. This is, after all, what breeding is all about.

However there is ample evidence that this is not always the case with Robins. Not only have divorces been recorded from year to year but also between the parents of successful first broods. Some of these went on to nest again, even later in the same breeding season, with different mates — and did so successfully! It seems likely that there is little to be gained, for a species with a short expectation of life, in trying to remain faithful to a mate from one season to another. This is because the chances of both surviving to the next season are not very high (see p. 38). However, if both do survive, it is quite possible that fidelity to the territory may have the effect of keeping pairs together.

Divorce in the course of the same breeding season is much less easy to explain. However, sometimes the parents have divided the fledged brood between themselves and each looks after its youngsters for about three weeks. Were one of the parents to lose its portion of the brood early during this period this could be a very good reason for divorce. The parent without any further responsibility could find a new mate; then a new breeding attempt could be made two weeks or more before it would be possible with the original partner. Since early breeding attempts are always likely to fledge more young than later attempts, this would be a very good way of passing on more of one's genes to the next generation. However it seems likely that most early broods are looked after by the male alone whilst the female gets on with the next clutch. The territorial behaviour of the adults gradually tails off during the breeding season and, at the same time, the food supply increases. Thus the disruption to territories that such divorces might precipitate is not too serious.

Bigamy

Almost all Robins are monogamous during the breeding season but there have been a few well documented cases of bigamy: who'd have believed it of Robins? It is quite easy to see how this can happen if two females approach the same male at the time when he is wishing to pair. Normally, of course, one or other of the females will take precedence and drive off the second and, in any case, the chances of two females making their approaches at the same time must be remote.

In two recorded cases of bigamy (a male with two females) each of the females actually held her own sub-territory within the area which the male defended and drove the other out of it. Since the female is responsible for nest-building the two nests were some distance apart and the nesting attempts were staggered. The male spent most of his time with one of the hens until she was sitting on eggs and then paid court to the other. In one instance, although the second nest was not found, the female was almost certainly incubating when the cock disappeared — perhaps it became too much of a strain for him. Almost immediately two new cocks appeared and paired, on the separate territories, with the females. In the other case one of the females was taken by a hawk before either clutch of eggs hatched.

However other sets of bigamous birds were much more cosy. In one case the two females built their nests in an ivy-covered wall in a Sussex garden — immediately above each other and only about 30cm apart. The records are not quite detailed enough to be able to work out whether the two clutches were laid at exactly the same time but both produced fledged young. Later a second brood was reared in the top nest. Far and away the most impressive example of togetherness (also from Sussex) was recorded in 1959. Two Robins laid in the same nest. The final clutch was 11 or 12 eggs and both birds were observed happily incubating side by side. The nest had an enlarged cup but sadly was eventually deserted. Some of the eggs were partly developed but it seems likely that they would not all have been properly warmed in such unusual circumstances.

Bigamy is a common strategy among some species of birds. In Britain, for instance, male Corn Buntings may even have more than two hens each. However it seems unlikely to be a good course of action for a species like the Robin where the male has such a major role to play in the breeding attempt. The provision of food for the female during the first half of the cycle and the feeding of the young, both in and out of the nest, would seem to require his full attention and not leave time for 'something on the side'. Indeed the conflicting demands on his time could be expected to cause *both* attempts to fail and so none of his genes would be made available for the following generations. Which all goes to support conventional anthropomorphic morality.

Incest

Our own human taboos and laws operate strongly against incestuous relationships — although some Freudian theory suggests that suppressed incestuous longings are highly significant in determining human behaviour patterns. In wild animal populations incestuous relationships can only be proved where individuals are recognizable, generally by being marked. Most people imagine that the young produced by pairings between close relatives are likely to be defective but, provided that inbreeding only happens infrequently, this is not necessarily the case. Indeed many island populations have probably arisen when a single pair of birds have managed to colonize the site, and many captive/domestic species are subject to inbreeding as a deliberate way of developing the strain.

Incestuous relationships were not discovered during David Lack's detailed investigations of Robins but two have been reported during long-term garden studies. One was described by Edwin Cohen, at Sway in Hampshire, who conducted very long-term studies on the birds in his garden using colour rings for individual identification. During 1961 a male reared the previous year paired with his mother. She died during the winter and for 1962 he paired with his sister (reared in the same brood). Both matings produced fledged young.

A few years later, also in Hampshire, there was another recorded pairing between mother and son. In this instance the circumstances were slightly artificial since the birds concerned were hand-tame in the observer's garden. This particular pairing was very successful. The first nest was built in February but attacked (2 eggs were taken) on the 15th. The second nest was completed a few days later and fledged one youngster from a clutch of four eggs and the hen had built her third nest before these had fledged. Four young were fledged from this nest early in May, a fourth one produced four young at the beginning of June and a final one a single youngster in July. Ted Sprackland, in whose garden this was all happening, was supplying extra food throughout by hand-feeding.

He also shepherded the young birds into a fruit cage, for their protection. Nevertheless the incestuous pair had produced ten youngsters in a season.

Even if incest is a *bad thing* it is difficult to see how a few chance incestuous pairings could be avoided. The spotty young Robin that emerges from the nest has a very different appearance and behaviour patterns from the red-breasted adult. It is difficult to see how a broodmate or parent would be able to recognize the transformed youngster in a later year — the brood will have broken up and dispersed long before the post-juvenile moult had transformed the young birds. The main mechanism for avoiding inbreeding is therefore likely to be the short-distance dispersal which mostly takes place during the bird's first autumn. Whilst it is only under conditions of intensive study that incestuous pairings will come to light, it may be no coincidence that both in Edwin Cohen's and Ted Sprackland's gardens the Robins were being fed regularly. This may have suppressed the urge to move away.

Nest sites

There can be few British birdwatchers and gardeners who have not seen a Robin's nest. The familiar structure has a hair-lined cup built on a foundation of moss on top of dead leaves. It is generally well concealed but may be out in the open within an otherwise safe site — as for instance on the shelf of a garden shed. Sometimes Robins choose bizarre, if cosy sites such as in the pockets of

This Robin innocently perched on a pile of logs is actually at its nest entrance — the tunnel between the logs opens out into a suitable chamber for the nest (see right, where a log has been removed).

gardening jackets; another favourite is in the back of a half-open drawer. However the nest in the wild is generally fairly difficult to find and may be very beautifully concealed in a more sensible place.

Undoubtedly the most frequent natural sites used are hollows, nooks and crannies behind ivy or other climbing plants growing on walls or trees; Robins also like hedge-banks or other situations where a fully concealed cavity can be occupied. In the old forests the raised tree-root discs from fallen forest giants provide sheltered holes and crevices for a nesting site which may have been the Robin's ancestral home in the ancient forests of thousands of years ago. There are a number of records of the Robin setting up home in the old hollow of a Blackbird or Song Thrush nest which was well concealed in vegetation. Some will also nest, at ground level, within tussocks of grass – I saw one at Cambridge which had been 'topped' by a rotary mower, leaving an open nest with young – they did not survive long.

Discarded human materials may offer considerable potential. What is junk to us can be Home Sweet Home to a Robin, and nests in kettles, paint-pots or other containers thrown carelessly away are common. Wrecked cars in scrap yards, piles of logs and tumble-down buildings are often used. Considerable inconvenience may be caused by birds nesting in letter-boxes. There was even an ambitious Robin that nested in the engine of a Mosquito aircraft at an RAF station in Gloucestershire – you'll be glad to know it was successful. Inconsiderately placed nests have been known to cause the machinery in factories to be switched off for the duration of breeding. One such incident occurred in 1952 when the birds nested (successfully) in semi-automatic brush-making machinery at the Kleen-e-ze works in Bristol: the machine was out of commission for about a month, and four young Robins were reared (in a nest made largely from bristle and hair-fibre).

Making a nest-box

The construction and siting of an open-fronted nest-box for a Robin is a fairly simple project. The cutting diagram illustrates how the box may be made, but quite often an existing container can be perfectly well modified and placed in a good position. Over the last two years five broods have been raised in my garden in an old enamelled kettle placed, for this purpose, in the fork of a mature and ivy-covered apple-tree.

Siting of the box is very important for the birds will not normally nest in an exposed position. Putting the box

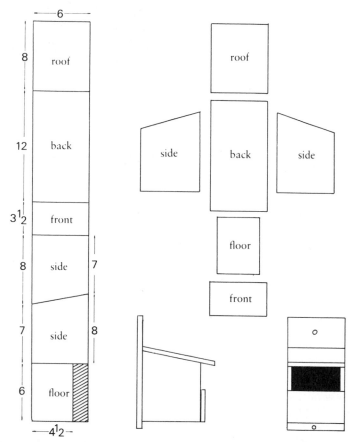

This diagram represents an ideal sort of nest-box for a Robin. The general idea of the box is what is important rather than the exact dimensions. Wood is so expensive nowadays that it is best to modify the design of the box to use what material is available rather than to spend a lot of money on the exact wood recommended – I find that damaged pallets are ideal as a source of material. Note: all measurements are in inches.

behind ivy, clematis, honeysuckle or any other climber is the best bet. The recommended height is about 150cm (5ft – shoulder-height) – an acceptable height for the Robins and generally out of reach of ground predators but still convenient for humans to see what is happening, perhaps with the aid of a box to stand on.

The same site may be used for successive broods without much tarting up of the old nest but, if you are lucky enough to attract a Robin to a nest-box, it is always a very good idea to offer one or two alternative sites for second broods. Over the winter it is also best to get rid of the old nest material as it may get damp and disgusting and it could be harbouring parasites. Protection of the vulnerable nest from cats may be provided by a generous covering of two inch mesh chicken wire enclosing the nest site some 50 or 70cm away from it – Robins can get through, but cat is thwarted. In sheds and other outhouses the Robin will readily gain access through a high window or broken roof where a cat may not be able to follow.

An ideal site for an open-fronted nest-box – partly concealed on a wall or fence where a climber is growing.

Speedy nest building

Although Rome was not built in a day, the Robin, when it is nesting, can get a substantial structure built in a very short period. The fastest on record was a nest in Basingstoke. Between break-fast and lunchtime an almost complete nest had been built in a gardener's coat pocket. The coat had been hung in the toolshed and, although history does not record what happened to the nest, I would not have given it much chance of success. The old-fashioned gardener was not renowned for his sentimentality or love of birds – particularly in the spring when the Blackbirds seem to insist on making their nests from newly planted out bedding subjects.

Another very fast nest proved suc-cessful. This bird, in Birmingham, started to build in an unmade bed whilst the legitimate occupant was having breakfast! In this instance the soft-hearted human left the birds alone and a brood was successfully reared. Robins seem to like beds in Birmingham as another built a nest in a cardboard box at the end of a bed. Young successfully fledged, the bed having been in normal use all the time. The bedroom windows were left open for the duration.

Finding nests

I am not the person to write about the finding of any bird nest — except those in nest-boxes — as I am one of the world's worst nest-finders. To excuse myself, the Robin's nest can be very difficult to find. However, studying some aspects of the Robin's behaviour can be a great help.

First of all the period of nest construction, although short, can give a very good opportunity of seeing where the nest is being built. A female seen to be gathering nesting material should be assiduously watched. During laying there is very little chance of discovering the nest but, as soon as the female starts to incubate, one's chances improve. The hen leaves the nest every quarter of an hour or so to feed herself and to be fed by the male. She uses the contact note (see p. 98) to stimulate him into bringing food and the soft, shimmering begging note whilst she is being fed. Hear this happening and you have a fairly good chance of watching where she goes back. The secret is not to charge straight in but to wait and watch her back again, even twice more, and then carefully approach the spot. Often it will be well concealed and gentle tapping of the vegetation with a twig should get her to leave and so reveal where the nest is. Often observation on the nest may easily be made using a mirror so that the vegetation is not disturbed — do be careful. Desertion of the nest is unlikely but predators may use the tracks you have made to find it.

Later on both parents may be watched taking food to the young — their feeding frequency is low when the young are small but increases quickly to once every 3-4 minutes at its peak. Some experts claim to be able to discover nests just by searching suitable sites. One has told me that he looks for the horizontal

pad of nest material that the adults use as a doorstep whilst cruising down country lanes in his car. I can believe him as I have seen the phenomenal totals of baby Robins he manages to ring — however it has *never* worked for me. Another expert nest-finder has explained that it is much easier to see a Robin's nest when the female is *not* sitting than when she is. Her plumage fills out the hole where the nest is but, if she is not sitting on her eggs, there will be a characteristic dark, globular shadow. This I can also believe and it is what you need to look for if you have disturbed a bird and cannot tell exactly where the nest is.

What, you may legitimately ask, is one doing trying to find a nest in the first place? The answer is — not just for fun. Those who fill in Nest Record Cards and who ring young Robins are producing the sort of information on which our knowledge of Robins is based. Proper, careful recording at the nest should not put it under any additional danger but the person looking must be very careful not to leave traces of his presence to act as clues for marauding corvids or cats. And do not try to remove the young from the nest. If you think you might damage the nest's surroundings you should leave it alone and, in any case, you should space out your visits; a daily visit is much too frequent.

A suitable schedule for a nest found whilst it is being built might be as shown on the Nest Record Card:

OBSERVER C.J.MEAD				SPECIES RobiN		YEAR 1983	B.T.O.Ref
NO. of EGGS or YOUNG at each visit.				Record here stage of building, if bird sitting, if eggs warm, age of young, ring nos. etc	COUNTY HERTS	If this record is entered on ATLAS CARD put ✓ in box	Office Use Only
DATE		G.M.T.	EGGS	YNG			
Day	Month						D
10	4	08	·	·	Nest almost complete	LOCALITY (place-name) TRING Grid Ref SP 91	C
15	4	19	3	·			
24	4	19	6	·	4 oft. Eggs hot.		H
3	5	08	·	6	Two days old	ALTITUDE above sea level 300 ft.	
8	5	19	·	6	7 Days — Ringed	HABITAT Delete those inapplicable RURAL/SUBURBAN/URBAN	F
14	5	08	·	✓	Large — No count.	Mature suburban	
16	5	13	·	·	Nearly fledged young in vicinity.	garden	
						NEST SITE Old Kettle in Ivy covered apple tree	
Further visits, notes on outcome, etc ON BACK					Height above ground or cliff base 5 ft		

The second visit, during laying, allows the date of the first egg to be calculated. Estimates of the ages of the young can also be used to confirm the nesting details or calculate them if the nest was not found and recorded in its early stages. Ringing takes place halfway through the fledging period when the chicks will readily settle back in the nest after handling.

Mobile homes

With an intensely territorial species, like the Robin, it comes as quite a surprise to find that successful nests have been built in, and young raised from, vehicles which have been moved during breeding. The most amazing was a nest, with young, in a Sussex railway wagon, which had to be moved over 100km. One of the parents made the journey (luckily a return one) and the young eventually fledged. In another instance the incubating female was taken for a journey on her nest in the engine compartment of a car. When the driver discovered the bird, on his return home, the car was laid up for the duration.

During the 1960s I spent a lot of my time each summer studying Sand Martins. This took me into many sand and gravel pits where the digging was done by large, noisy but slow-moving drag-line excavators. Several of these had Pied Wagtail nests tucked away in the works — often in the box containing the drum on which the control cables were wound. Twice Robins successfully used the same site and once a pair nested in the lorry used to take the excavated material from the sand-face to the washing plant. This entailed a regular journey of about 200m many times each day, although, in this case,

the lorry was always parked overnight and at weekends in the same place. Being of no fixed abode seemed not to trouble the Robins over much, and both nests were successful. Perhaps the problem of defending a mobile territory was lessened by the fact that a sandpit is hardly a desirable Robin residence, so there weren't too many competitors about.

Mobility may, of course, work to the Robin's advantage. If a nest is inconveniently sited but in something which can be moved it is quite possible to persuade the birds to follow the displaced nest. It is best to try to put the nest back into a similar position; if for instance, part of a heap of bricks in which Robins are nesting has to be moved, the birds may take to the nest if it is replaced a few metres further back in the stack. Success is most likely if the nest is conspicuously marked for a day or two before the move — for instance by placing brightly coloured polythene near it — and then the marker and the nest are shifted. The bird has more chance of realizing what has happened. Such moves are generally more likely to succeed if the parents are feeding chicks rather than if the eggs are still being incubated.

Confused nests

In nature 'large' structures are seldom symmetrical, although 'small' ones — flowers, leaves, snowflakes, for example — often are. The Robin in the wild therefore seldom has to face the problems posed by man, who often builds large and very symmetrical structures, with repeated openings for the Robin to nest in. These can cause confusion to Robins unaccustomed to regularity. It may be bad enough for a bird to have two similar shelves in a garden-shed — two nests may be started, but generally the bird will fix on one in which to lay its clutch. However there are other instances which should, by rights, have led to terminal nervous breakdown for the unfortunate birds concerned.

Several times Robins have been found breeding in stacks of pipes or crates which afforded no easy visual references: the whole lot looked the same. In the worst case 23 different nest starts were made by the same exhausted pair. Other birds have used the regularly spaced niches within the wall of a sewage farm filter bed and got as far as laying partial clutches in three different homes. Another hen started 16 nests in different pigeon-holes in a workshop but eventually mastered the problem of telling one from another and in the end only completed one nest. She laid her clutch and reared the young successfully.

Any sympathetic human, who realizes that a bird is being confused by this conundrum can easily provide the solution. All you need do is make a conspicuous break in the symmetry — block off one of the pipes, turn around a crate or simply put something obvious in one of the pigeon-holes — any would be sufficient to give the bird a good visual clue: a sort of signpost to latch on to. (We have the same problem driving round new towns or council estates. All the roads look the same and soon we are confused and certain we've 'been down this way before'. After a while we learn to tell one road from another by the cars parked on it or we recognize one house from the others by its mauve front door.)

Robin eggs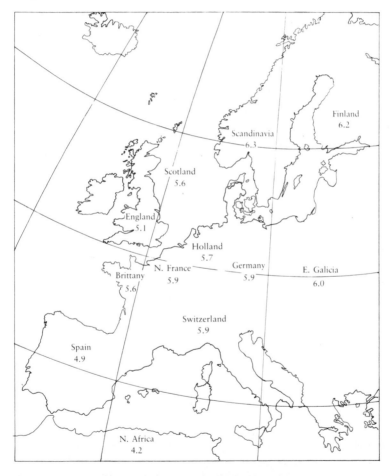

Robin eggs are quite variable in terms of amount of colour. All have a pure
white ground colour and a speckling of reddish or reddish-brown spots —
occasionally these are missing and the eggs are pure white; other times, when
the marks are particularly thick, the egg may look wholly reddish. A few eggs
have the marks confined to the wide end so that the egg appears to have a
reddish cap.

Finland
6.2

Scandinavia
6.3

Scotland
5.6

England
5.1

Holland
5.7

N. France
5.9

Germany
5.9

E. Galicia
6.0

Brittany
5.6

Switzerland
5.9

Spain
4.9

N. Africa
4.2

*Data gathered from a variety of sources shows that the clutch size of
breeding Robins varies; northern and eastern birds lay bigger clutches than
southern and western ones. Re-drawn from Lack, British Birds, 39.*

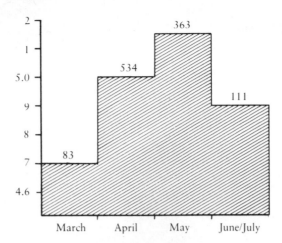

In Britain the average size of Robin clutches increases from March through April to reach a peak in May – late nests are again lower. This chart was based on counts of more than a thousand clutches (numbers on top of each column).

A great deal is known about the number of eggs laid in a clutch. In Britain about 80% of clutches contain either 5 or 6 eggs with 4, 7, 3 and 8 the next most frequent. But clutch sizes vary geographically. Averages for different populations are shown on the map on the previous page – the minimum being 4.2 eggs for North African populations and the maximum 6.3 in Scandinavia. Numbers seem to be larger in the North as opposed to the South and also in the East as opposed to the West. Similar variations are known for some other species and the main difference between north and south is probably associated with lower overall survival rates in higher latitudes.

As well as the changes that operate regionally there is also a change in average clutch size through the breeding season. In Britain March nests have the lowest average number of eggs and May ones the highest – although the changes are small: from 4.7 to 5.15 eggs (see figure). Similar variations have been found for other populations too. David Lack suggested that the increasing day-length, and thus extra time available for the parents to feed the young, may be responsible for this seasonal change.

Of course there are many losses between the laying of the clutch of eggs and the appearance of fledged young. Many nests are found by predators and destroyed: others fail because of the weather or the death of the female and so do not contribute any hatched young at all. A lot of these total failures seem to occur in suburban areas, and the nests that are particularly successful often come from the most rural sites – the comparative figures are 40% and over 80%. Even where young had successfully hatched there were further failures before fledging – ranging from 5% to 40%. Overall, from very detailed studies in many parts of Britain, 73% of the eggs from completed clutches hatched into chicks and 78% of these survived to leave the nest. Thus the overall success rate, from an egg in a completed clutch to fledged youngster, was rather less than 57%.

Basket of eggs

The female Robin's clutch of eggs is generally kept within reasonable bounds. The birds have evolved a maximum clutch that is the most that a single female can keep properly warm during incubation. For the Robin this seems to be 7 although a very few 8-egg clutches are 100% successful. Egg collectors, by milking a nest – that is taking the freshly laid egg from an incomplete clutch each day – have often been able to induce hens to lay 10 or 11 eggs. There is however one amazing female that lost control. She nested in a strawberry basket in a garage in Kent during May 1944 and laid three batches of eggs, with a short gap between each 'clutch', ending with a total of 20. Unfortunately, at this juncture, she was disturbed by a cat and had not started to incubate. The observer noted that the eggs were three deep in the nest and the Robin had some difficulty in balancing herself on the pile when she came to lay another!

The long wait

Female Robins have a fairly standard length of time to sit on their nests: few have longer than a fortnight to wait before their eggs hatch. But, some unfortunate females who sit on infertile clutches do not seem to know when to call it a day. There are several records of these poor birds incubating, in vain, for more than twice the normal span. One lasted for 5 weeks and the record is 48 days! Eventually the frustrated bird will desert the nest but, if I come across such a tragedy, I always feel that it is kindest to destroy the clutch and allow the female some respite from her vigil.

The Cuckoo in the nest

The Cuckoo is the only brood parasite of Robins in Europe. The female Cuckoo lays an egg in the Robin's nest, generally removing one of the Robin's eggs at the same time. Although the Cuckoo is much bigger than the Robin its egg is small in relation to its body size and the incubation period is short: the egg is similar in size to the Robin's and hatches as quickly. The newly hatched Cuckoo ejects the eggs or other chicks from the nest so that it can monopolize its host's attentions during a period of about three weeks in the nest. Whilst it is being fed in the nest its exceptionally brightly coloured orange gape and noisy and insistent calls act as a super stimulus for the adult birds to feed it. Quite often other birds nesting nearby will give it food they have collected as they pass the nest. To be successfully reared a young Cuckoo needs all the insect food that would have been fed to a whole brood of the host species − and then some.

What the parent Robins may have seen when the young Cuckoo had failed to throw out their youngsters.

In Central Europe and parts of Russia the Robin is a very important host and the Cuckoos there have developed a very close egg mimicry. This lessens the chance of the Robin realizing that a Cuckoo has laid in its nest and either removing the alien egg or deserting the nesting attempt. Even as close as France some studies have found up to 13% of all Cuckoo's eggs in Robins' nests; in Britain the British Trust for Ornithology (BTO) had reports from its 'nest recorders' that only about 2% of 606 Cuckoo's eggs were in Robins' nests. By far the most common host was the Dunnock, with 53%, followed by the Reed Warbler and Meadow Pipit, with 14% each. The Robin led the 23 'also rans' which included such unsuitable species as Linnet, Greenfinch and Skylark, which are seed-eaters: food ignored by any properly brought-up Cuckoo.

The analysis of BTO records showed that only 0.4% of all the Robin's nests

In flight the Cuckoo can look very like a hawk.

reported upon had been parasitized by Cuckoos. The figures for other hosts were much higher — Dunnock 2.2%, Reed Warbler 3.0%, Meadow Pipit 3.1%, PiedWagtail 0.7%, Rock Pipit 3.6% and Tree Pipit 1.0%. The analysis also checked which species were preferred in what habitat, and this revealed that Robins were comparatively important in certain habitats. The Robin turned out to be second only to the Dunnock in woodland, third to Dunnock and Pied Wagtail in the vicinity of buildings and third to Meadow Pipit and Dunnock on lowland heaths.

Tremendous controversy waged in the early part of the century as to exactly how the female Cuckoo managed to get her egg into a semi-enclosed nest like that of the Robin. One faction was certain that the Cuckoo first laid the egg outside the nest and later picked it up, in her bill, and inserted it. This is wrong and probably arose because the actions of the Cuckoo at the nest are so very fast and a glimpse of the unfortunate host's egg in the female's bill put people on the wrong track. In fact she lays it directly, almost squirting it into the nest, and does not make any attempt to adjust its position, even if it is not wholly in the nest. Incidentally Cuckoo's eggs have a slightly thicker shell than other eggs of the same size and are unlikely to suffer damage during their first flight!

Before it is ready to leave the nest the young Cuckoo overflows its surroundings.

Generally the host does not recognize that anything is wrong but sometimes eggs are thrown out by the rightful owner. If the Cuckoo is surprised at the nest in the act of laying the breeding attempt may be abandoned completely. Cuckoos are, of course, exceptionally able nest-finders — their survival depends on this ability. They can spend a long time concealed in cover watching and waiting for a suitable host to give away its nest site. If she finds a nest with young the female Cuckoo may destroy the whole nest to make available the replacement nest that the unfortunate hosts will build for her own egg. Most female Cuckoos have a preferred host species and this will be the one in whose nest they were reared and whose eggs are closest to the ones the Cuckoo herself produces — obviously the genes which control egg colour pass along the female line.

A few hours after the young Cuckoo has hatched, it starts ejecting its competitors from the nest; this behaviour lasts for about three days or until there is nothing left to throw out. The effort needed is extraordinary. The young bird backs to the side of the nest balancing the egg or chick in a hollow between its 'shoulder blades'. It may have to try time and time again. Often the egg or chick does not fall right out of the nest but remains on the edge — ignored by the parents. Sometimes the Cuckoo itself falls out and perishes and rarely, with two Cuckoo's eggs in a single nest, a battle develops: just occasionally both remain in the nest and are reared together.

In one exceptional nest a clutch of five Robins (with a Cuckoo egg) were watched carefully. The Robins hatched on June 4th (only four — one was infertile) and the Cuckoo emerged the following day. It tried, as usual, to eject the young but failed — probably because of the enclosed nature of the nest. Eventually the Cuckoo settled down on top of its unexpected brood partners and fledged normally after 20 days. Amazingly the young Robins had been able to obtain enough food to keep alive and they left the nest three days later. This is roughly ten days later than normal.

The strain placed on this gallant pair of parent Robins can only be imagined. The young Cuckoo takes all the food that it can get and gains weight at roughly the same rate as an entire normal brood of Robins would. Detailed studies on Reed Warblers show the weight gain of the young Cuckoo is almost exactly the same as an average brood of four young warblers until the eighth day. At this stage — at about 11g each — the young Reed Warblers slow down in their weight gain but the Cuckoo carries on at the same rate until it reaches roughly 70g at 13 days. In fact the Reed Warbler- and Dunnock-raised Cuckoos which have been studied do not seem to have done as well as the single Cuckoo raised by Robins weighed regularly in Oxford during 1947. This bird fledged at over 100g on the 19th or 20th day whereas the average Reed Warbler-reared bird only just exceeded 80g and a single Dunnock-hosted youngster fledged at 85g

Following fledging the young Cockoo is in a very vulnerable state for it is not capable of confident flight and sits around begging for food with a very piercing and noisy squealing. This is the time when almost any adult with food will forget its own young and stuff its load down the Cuckoo's throat. The frantic foster parents are dwarfed by 'their' chick and quite often land on its back and, by bending over and forwards, feed it without having to find an inanimate perch!

Naturally the human observer has great sympathy with the host species when a parasitized nest is found. However the evolution of brood parasitism as a breeding strategy is quite 'natural' and is practised by other species quite unrelated to the Cuckoo. It would be wrong to interfere in the struggle but it is absolutely fascinating to watch the outcome.

Tit Robins?

The usual kinds of nestbox that we put up in the garden are of two basic designs. Robins prefer to use the 'open-fronted' type, where they can sit on the nest and easily see out. The other sort of box, with only a tiny entrance, is mainly favoured by tits.

Every year I visit almost 2,000 ordinary tit-style nestboxes. These have small round holes for the birds to enter and have been put up in woods and gardens for Great, Blue and Coal Tits and, in Wales and Hereford, they are also used by Pied Flycatchers. The standard hole size is roughly 30mm diameter, the size of a 10p piece, and I have never found a Robin breeding in any of them. Even Redstarts, which regularly use the boxes, prefer to have a rather bigger diameter entrance, and

they are quite often found in boxes with holes enlarged by squirrels or wood-peckers.

However I was amazed to discover that Robins in small numbers regularly use this type of box in southern Sweden. Over a period of 8 years 7 of 1,262 breeding attempts in these boxes were made by Robins. Admittedly the boxes had a slightly wider entrance (35mm) but clearly the Swedish Robins were exploiting a nest site that no British bird would even think about. Such a box is a very well protected site for a nesting bird and it was shown that the box nesters were particularly successful at raising young – I wonder if the habit will spread and if British Robins will eventually start to compete with the tits and flycatchers?

Natural food

Anyone who has watched a Robin feeding in natural surroundings – whether in wild woodland or the garden shrubbery – will realize that it uses a standard technique most of the time. Where suitable low perches exist, it will watch for prey items from the perch, dart down to the ground, pick up the food and fly

A Robin on the lawn, like this, is looking – not listening – for worms.

back up again. If it is feeding in the open, where there are no perches, the bird will hop quickly forward and pause in an upright position before darting forward to take its food. This is often interpreted as the bird 'listening for a worm' but, almost certainly, the Robin is using visual clues and not sound. The worm is likely to cause the blades of grass to move as it displaces the roots underground. Obviously worms are not available for Robins in dry weather since they will be well out of the birds' reach in the deeper damp soil, but in wet weather worms provide a juicy feast.

So Robins feed mainly on insects and other arthropods. Almost any little creepy crawly will do – beetles, caterpillars, ants, flies, spiders, centipedes, maggots, snails, earthworms, etc. Otherwise the birds may take vegetable foods like berries, grains and seeds – which even form a major part of the diet at certain times of the year. As is to be expected, for a common species, all sorts of peculiar foods are recorded in Robin literature. For instance birds beside streams and ponds have been recorded as taking mosquito larvae, damselflies, dragonflies, whirligig beetles, tadpoles, minnows and even young roach. This last was taken by a bird which dived into the water – Robins are distantly related to Dippers after all! One bird was recorded taking young sand lizards – now wholly illegal under the Wildlife and Countryside Act. Another was found catching worker bees and skilfully discarding the sting. Several have been seen following burrowing moles across a field to feed on the items turned up in the animal's hills.

Vegetable food is particularly important to Robins during the autumn, winter and early spring. Fruit is readily taken both from the garden (currants, raspberries, etc.) and from the wild (blackberries, haws, rowan, bilberry, elder, yew, etc.). Studies of wintering birds in southern Spain provided very unexpected results. Many of the birds were doing exactly what had been predicted – feeding on a mixture of animal and vegetable food, the latter mostly pulpy fruits. In fact a very large proportion of the animal food was ants and the fruits which were most commonly taken were those of the Lentisk, the Strawberry Tree, Portuguese Laurel and *Phillyrea latifolia*. These birds faced

difficulties in the late winter when their food supply was significantly depleted. However, another population living in oak woods was taking considerable amounts of acorn flesh. They were unable to get at it themselves but had to find acorns which had been crushed or already part-eaten. In the study area this was mostly by Nuthatches or Great Tits. In December these Robins were taking almost 80% (by volume) acorn flesh in their diet — and they were doing very well. In fact their weights were significantly higher than the birds in cultivated areas and their fat reserves were much better.

Some other detailed studies, by Marion East in Sussex, have shown differences in male and female feeding behaviour. Marion East colour-ringed her birds so that she knew them individually and recorded their feeding behaviour in different weather conditions. She observed that males spent less time in each bout of feeding on the ground when it was warmer (6°-10°C) than when it was colder (0°-5°C), and they also changed perch more frequently during cold conditions. Also, in warm weather, the males spent more time looking around from their perches than they did during cold periods. Females showed no significant differences with temperature.

As might be expected, since cold weather reduces the activity of their prey, both sexes of Robin fed more on the ground in the colder periods than the warmer ones: when the prey is inactive, Robins must get closer to see where they are, rather than spotting movement from afar. These differences may have evolved to reduce competition between the sexes. However it would only be useful where the pairs have already formed and breeding territories occupied in the winter for otherwise the males and females defend their own territories. Alternatively they may possibly reflect an additional territorial drive in the males when the weather is mild: extra time on the look-out may enable them to spot intruders more quickly.

Robins in cold weather

Undoubtedly the most desperate time for Robin survival happens, in Britain, every few years when we have a severe winter. During mild winters most Robins are easily able to find enough food to survive — provided that they hold a good territory in a suitable area. When really cold weather strikes all sorts of problems arise and many birds may die. For instance, in mid-December 1981 the exceptionally cold weather led to almost four times as many ringing recoveries as usual.

The problems are all to do with food and shelter. The cold weather comes at a time of year when there is the least daylight and so the birds have only a short time each day when they can see to feed. Snow may cover many suitable feeding areas and bury food supplies that would otherwise have been available. Severe cold weather cools the birds, who must find sheltered places to roost in and, in any case, will almost certainly have to eat more food to provide metabolic heat for survival. The cold weather will also drive many of the small arthropods on which the Robins feed to hide in nooks and crannies where the birds are unable to reach them.

What can we do to help? Obviously not much for a Robin with a territory in the country, far from any human habitation, and such birds will have to do their best to survive. This will often involve teaming up with other birds or animals that are able to scrape the snow away. In the woods near Tring the territorial Robins often use the areas scraped clear of snow by the Fallow Deer. In other places they may feed on tracks or roads or even follow grazing cattle or walking men — any tiny clearance of snow is a potential feeding site.

Near human habitations Robins often do very well at bird-tables. This is the time of the year when Robins will become tame most easily, as it is the time of the year when they rely on us most. It is no coincidence that the first sightings of Robins hovering at and taking peanuts from hanging bags have often been during cold spells. Once they have learnt the behaviour they will, of course, continue to use it. However peanuts are probably not ideal food unless they are shredded or crushed. The method used to produce the Robin's favourite food at the bird-table — mealworms — is given elsewhere (p. 106). However all sorts of food will happily be taken from feeding stations and kitchen scraps (particularly

meaty ones), fat, cheese, cake and breadcrumbs and dried fruit are all eaten with relish. All are a valuable supplement to the meagre supply of natural food available at this time.

As with many species which spend the winter with us in Britain, the Robin builds up a store of fat during the winter. This is used as insurance for when weather conditions deteriorate and it is probably possible for a Robin, in good condition at mid-winter, to survive several days without having to take in much (if any) food. The problem is, of course, that most severe spells last for many days and a foolish Robin, trying to sit it out, may find the conditions are still poor when it runs out of reserves. Analysis of the ringing recoveries during winter shows that most are found during the second week of a cold spell. During cold snaps, Robins will always try to feed unless the weather is so bad that they might die of exposure.

Why spades?

One of the traditional pictures of the tame Robin shows it perching on a gardener's spade. Why does it do it so often? The answer is simple. The Robin's preferred feeding technique is to use a low perch to survey an area and then to fly down to take any prey it sees. The spade is an ideal perch. Add to this the presence of the gardener, turning the soil and exposing such useful food as earthworms, leatherjackets and other grubs. Heaven for any garden Robin!

Communal roosts

Until recently it was thought that Robins always roosted singly (or as a pair during the breeding season) in their territories. However ringers who were netting Blackbird roosts in the Aberdeen area during the early 1970s started to catch many more than just their local Robins. They realized that they had found a site where Robins were roosting communally. Previously the only such roosts that had been reported were on islands during migration periods when large numbers of migrant Robins were resting.

In all they discovered six roosting sites where they caught between 6 and 22 Robins during a single evening. The biggest roost held 53 different individuals through the season and the smallest 13. The roosts were first used in September and the peak of occupation was in October and November with another, smaller increase in February. By ringing the birds in the roosts with different colours, it was discovered that they were holding territories during the day in nearby housing estates where they were getting food from the householders. It seemed likely that the birds came from breeding territories in local woodlands – hence the peak in roost numbers as the autumn and spring territories were set up. The autumn territories may not have provided any suitable roosting sites and most did not hold breeding birds – probably due to the lack of nest sites. Investigation of data from other ringers revealed that a few similar, though smaller, roosts might exist in several parts of Britain.

Robin song

Undoubtedly one of the most endearing characteristics of the Robin to its human admirers is its song. A distinctive, cheerful and varied warble given throughout the year, it has come to be a sound valued only slightly less than the Nightingale's more spectacular and richer notes. In any case the Nightingale is a rather rare summer migrant to south eastern parts of Britain, whereas the Robin

s common throughout almost the whole country. Also the Nightingale confines
ts singing to the month of May and a few days of June — contrary to common
belief, it also sings during the day as well as at night.

Robin song lasts almost all the year round. The birds not only use it to
advertise for mates in the spring but also to signal the presence of a defended
territory right through the year. The only time of year when it may be absent, or
at least much diminished, is during July, when the breeding season has ended
and the birds have not completed their moult. Even then, in late breeding
seasons, the very last spring songs from breeding males may be given at the
same time that the most precocious youngsters start their winter strains.

There are two distinctive songs. The first, the winter song, starts as early as
July when the first juveniles have completed their moult and is taken up by the
adults when they have finished theirs. It is used by male and female alike to
mark out and defend their autumn and winter territories. It has a less *bravura*
strain to it than the male's spring song — softer, more watery and generally a
little suppressed and introverted. This is despite the undoubted fact that the
defence of territory at this time of year is really important to the birds. In mid-
December, at the earliest, the first males will start their full-blooded spring song
that is both a confident expression of territorial ownership, designed to
intimidate any other Robin that dares to approach, and also a powerful
advertisement for a female. While they are paired females very seldom sing at
all.

For a few moments — or minutes — on a few days in the year the male
Robin's song may become a violent war chant. If an intruder dares to face up to
the owner and a real fight is in prospect, the intensity of song reaches dizzy
heights and Robins physically joined in combat will scream song phrases as
insults between themselves. The victor will often mark his ascendancy with a
particularly loud burst of triumphant song. Few who watch and listen to such
an encounter can have any doubt as to the importance of its song to the
victorious bird.

The structure of the Robin's song has been the subject of many investigations.
Interest was initially from the musical and aesthetic viewpoint and there are
many references in poetry and literature to the effect on humans of the bird's
song. Very interesting research work, notably by a French ornithologist, Dr
Brémond, has revealed something of the complexity of the song structure and its
meaning to the birds themselves. Although people like the idea that the birds are
speaking some form of language to each other with the different phrases making
up the words, in fact the Robin's song does not work like that at all. As we shall
see later, the calls do have fairly precise meanings but the complex songs are
sending general messages.

When a Robin sings it utters a string of short bursts of song, each lasting two
or three seconds, with short pauses between them. A bout of singing may last
several minutes and consist of dozens of bursts of song each of which will
contain a number of different motifs — typically four to six — which last, on

*Most Robins sing from within cover
and not from an exposed perch.*

average, about half a second each. Extensive research work has established that
an individual Robin may use several hundred basic motifs and is capable of
altering them through improvisation. Brémond documented more than 1,300
different motifs used by the Robins which he studied. He established that each
successive burst of song differed from the one before, that within each burst the
motifs were all different and that successive motifs were of higher and lower
pitch – roughly above and below 4kHz. This result showed how a very diverse
micro-structure within the bird's song could become strongly specific – and
recognizable to humans – with the imposition of only a few simple rules.

Further work was based on the experimental imitation of artificial Robin song
– first reconstituted bits of real Robin song: these showed, for example, that song
made up of only high- or low-pitched motifs produced reaction from the Robin
to whom they were played just over half the times they were played, whereas
mixed pitch song, made up in the same way from recorded motifs, produced
reaction in 88% of experiments. Other examples were based on electronically
synthesized sounds like Robin song; pure sine-wave sound – a very simple tone
– even when chopped into high and low sections, produced very little response.
Then more complex tones were added and the Robins exposed to the newly
manufactured sounds began to respond better. The experiments showed that the
Robin's song contains a great deal of redundant information within a very
characteristic formation which allows us (and Robins) to recognize that a
particular songster is a Robin on the basis of even the incomplete hearing of a
part of a burst of song. Even though the songs can be highly variable, it is quite
likely that adjacent birds get to know each other's song and so do not 'waste'
time on violent response to a familiar neighbour when a newcomer, singing in
the same position, would warrant a 'red alert'.

The intensity of the Robin's song varies through the year; it is at its height
when territories are being formed or are under dispute during the early autumn
and winter. Another noisy time is when the males begin their breeding song and
are attempting to gain mates but then, unless there are other Robins against

whom the territory must be defended, when paired, song tends to drop away. However there is one important burst of song for a few days from the male when the young have fledged. This may have two purposes. The first is, of course, to reinforce the pair bond and to encourage the female into another nesting attempt. However this is not the whole story since males at the end of the breeding season will also start to sing and it seems that they are teaching their offspring what Robin song is all about. Although there are clear differences between the winter and spring songs each is clearly Robin song and the youngsters seem to be able to learn from either. Certainly Robins that have been reared in captivity away from adults able to sing may develop into very poor songsters or even learn phrases from other species.

Unlike many species which sing from the top of a very conspicuous song-post — for instance Blackbirds, Song and Mistle Thrushes — Robins commonly sing from a concealed perch within a bush or tree. Often precisely the same spot is used time after time when there are apparently huge numbers of other suitable places in the vicinity. Sometimes Robins have been known to sing from conspicuous perches (particularly desperate unpaired males during the breeding season) and they have even been seen to sing in flight and whilst perched on the ground.

The Robin's vocal repertoire is, of course, not confined to song. There are several well known calls which have a very definite meaning to other Robins. For instance the begging call used both by the female when she is fed by the male and by nestlings begging for food — this is a shimmering, high-pitched hissing sound very characteristic of the species but not easy to locate. The alarm and roosting calls, the familiar 'tic, tic, tic', can be heard in response to many dangers and the fairly close presence of predators. If the predators come very close the rate of the 'tic, tic, tic' will speed up and it may become almost explosive in intensity like a clockwork key. This harsh alarm may be hurled at an inquisitive cat, rat or human, coming close to the nest, from what seems like a suicidally close approach but is often successful in distracting the predator's attention. Another signal, used for conveying alarm to a mate or the chicks, is the very thin high-pitched 'tseeeeeeep' used near the nest — an even more difficult call to locate.

This vocabulary of calls is, in many respects, quite similar to other species found in the same habitat. The evolution of similar calls obviously has a considerable benefit to all the species when it allows them to understand alarms for different sorts of common predators. This is particularly clearly shown when a roosting owl is discovered and many of the local birds join together to mob it. This draws the attention of them all to a potential predator and, in most cases, eventually causes the owl to move away and roost somewhere else. Not so much a trouble shared but a potential danger shifted to the territory of some other unfortunate bird.

Song at night

There are a number of birds that regularly sing at night — especially when there is moonlight, although some will carry on in total darkness. The most characteristic is the Nightingale but, without a doubt, the most common night-time songster in the towns and gardens areas of Britain is the Robin. There have been dozens of reports, often from impossible times of the year, like mid-winter, of Nightingales singing — which have turned out to be Robins. Indeed it could have been a Robin and not a Nightingale that was singing in Berkeley Square. Not only do Nightingales have a very short song-period, but they are all well south of the Sahara for the winter.

Nightingale, Luscinia megarhynchus.

In almost all cases such birds have been affected by street lighting, floodlights at marshalling yards or the strong lights used in some glass houses to induce flowering or fruiting of plants at an unnatural time of the year. The floodlights at an open-air theatre have more than once induced the local Robin to provide an unusual commentary on Shakespeare. Within aviaries Robins regularly carry on singing until the lights are put out and, once or twice, birds wintering within churches have been known to provide a melodious accompaniment to the midnight mass at Christmas.

In all these cases the Robins sang at night because of artificial light. Indeed in some cases the birds have been seen to feed — on the insects attracted to the light. In July 1973 in Liverpool a pair of Robins fed their nearly fledged brood of six young until well after dark (2200 GMT). They fed on moths caught at the lamps and also among the illuminated flowerbeds beside the road. In this case the entrance to the nest was also partly illuminated (perhaps the birds were suffering from insomnia) and I think it is doubtful that the parents would have taken food to the nest if this had not been the case. The late Derek England also reported (in the same issue of *British Birds*) that he regularly encountered

feeding Robins as early as 0500 hours, even in winter, feeding on and beside roads under sodium street lights in Norfolk.

Nocturnal song is not invariably associated with artificial lighting. A Robin suddenly awakened may burst into song — as happened during the bombardment of Monte Cassino in Italy during March 1944; it also happened when Robins were disturbed by anti-aircraft guns in several parts of England during the war, and when birds were disturbed by bombs in the Blitz. Even other birds may cause Robins to sing at odd hours — I have several times heard Robins singing at night where there have been a lot of Nightingales singing at full blast and, once, a quick burst of Robin song after I had disturbed a Pheasant which, in its turn, had blundered into the Robin's roosting place.

The Robin is one of the earliest birds to start the dawn chorus and one of the latest to stop singing in the evening. A study in South Wales by Adrian Wood showed that his local Robin consistently started to sing about half an hour before local sunrise for most of the year and even earlier at mid-summer. This was despite the fact that high ground to the east of his house meant that the actual time of sunrise was rather later than the standard quoted in the almanacks. For most of July and the early part of the winter the first calls were not song but alarms. There seems to be a very slight relationship between the time of the Robin's awakening and the clemency of the weather: not surprisingly Robins, like humans, prefer to stay abed when the weather is bad. Wind-speed and temperature have the greatest influence, although all activities may be suppressed in very wet weather.

Why call?

The range of calls used by Robins includes some with very obvious functions – for instance the angry alarms uttered round the head of a marauding cat or screamed at a roosting owl. There are others which seem to have a simple purpose – like the contact calls used by juveniles to keep in touch with their parents and the female with her mate. However, Robin communication may be more subtle, with the frequency and timing of calling involving strategies of bluff and double bluff.

For example, the contact call given by the female may be speeded up so that the male provides extra food for her. Detailed observations show that the parent Robins generally feed their young at a standard rate and so this strategy would not help the fledged youngster. The contact calls from fledglings are therefore given at a fairly constant rate – frequent enough for their parents not to lose them but not so frequent that they give away their presence to predators.

The two alarms – a thin, drawn-out 'tseep' for avian predators and a sharp 'tic' for ground predators – are used in different ways during the course of each breeding attempt. The 'tseep' alarm is given by males to warn their mates on the nest but they seldom 'tic'. Later, when the young have hatched, the rate of alarm calling increases rapidly and it is obvious that the adults use it to warn the youngsters. The 'tseep' alarm is still most frequently used, even when it is humans that are approaching an occupied nest. However 'tics' are also elicited by the time the young are about to leave the nest. Whilst the young are dependent on their parents it is worth the adult's while to ensure that its progeny have a better chance of survival by alarm calling – even if it puts the old birds at a slight risk. In fact, when the whole family 'tics' at once, life becomes very complicated for a predator which is trying to find them – a whole battery of identical 'tics' coming from half a dozen places at once.

It has been suggested, for some species with particularly loud and conspicuous begging calls, that the youngsters are 'daring' their parents to ignore them. If they carry on the calls may attract a predator and cause the parents to lose all the investment that they had put into the raising of the young to that age. The parents are being blackmailed into providing food for their offspring. This does not seem to be the case with the Robin, but the appalling noise that the young Cuckoo often makes, both in and out of the nest, may be a case in point. The poor Robin parents behave like frantic human parents who are forced to buy ice cream as a bribe to quieten a very badly behaved child!

The Robin's toilet

It has amazed many people to find that their birds immediately bathe in the drinking water that they put out in cold weather. Indeed Robins have been recorded bathing in freezing conditions shortly before going to roost in mid-winter, seemingly a sure way of catching their death of cold. This is probably a measure of the importance of keeping the plumage in good condition for survival in cold weather. The insulation provided by feathers and the layers of air trapped in them is well-known — after all that is why we use duck-feathers in the very best *eider*downs.

Robins use two main methods for keeping their feathers in good condition. They preen themselves fairly frequently using both their bills and feet to groom their feathers. This not only removes bits of dust but also ensures that the hooks on the individual plumes on each feather engage correctly: try for yourself on an old feather. The bill is used to transfer oils from the uropygial gland (on the Christmas Turkey this is the parson's nose) to the plumage. Many external parasites are dislodged or eaten during this process, along with bits of dirt, broken feathers, scurf and other debris. They also freshen up the plumage by dust or water-bathing. The action is to fluff out the feathers and work the dust or water in, like having a bath, to remove dirt, and therefore to improve the insulation which the feathers provide. Some birds go in for total immersion but others may have a good bathe in the dew or rain drops on foliage or other vegetation: some birds regularly bathe in falling rain — a natural shower.

Plumage maintenance during the winter is particularly important since the feathers growing during the autumn moult have to last through for a whole year. Not only does the bird depend upon the body plumage for insulation during the winter nights but it must also maintain the flight feathers in good condition. Any small bird with impaired powers of flight will have little chance of survival: it will surely quickly succumb to a predator.

Anting

Anting behaviour has been recorded for quite a range of birds, including several Robins. The birds appear to derive great pleasure from rubbing ants, held in the beak, through their plumage. In particular they use preening actions to draw the ants along the main wing feathers and through the underwing coverts. This is rather different from 'passive' anting recorded for other species which simply squat amongst the ants and let them crawl over their plumage. Various species of ant have been used, including the yellow garden ant (Lasius) and the bigger Formica species, and, in one case involving a Robin, Acanthomyops niger.

The only rational explanation which has been suggested is that the actions help to maintain the bird's plumage in good condition. The theory is that parasites may be driven out by the formic acid which the ants produce. However, everyone who has witnessed anting has been most impressed by the apparent pleasure that the birds always seem to derive from the activity – they become totally ecstatic – so perhaps they are simply getting the avian equivalent of being turned on. Or is it like a sauna – engrossing in progress and good when it stops?

Aggression to images in mirrors

Many species of bird have been observed attacking their own reflections in mirrors or other shiny surfaces. Corvids, wagtails, Chaffinches, even a Capercaillie, have spent hours, days or even weeks attacking hub-caps, wing-mirrors and car or house windows. And yet the ultra-aggressive Robin does not do it often — or does it?

In fact Robins probably respond to their images quite frequently, but their immediate aim in life is not to assault but to dominate the intruder — the image — and this is best achieved by getting onto a perch *above* the upstart. Then, of course, the intruder will immediately disappear for there is no longer a direct reflection of the owner in the surface. The image will only continue to irritate if there are no suitable higher perches and it is then that the rather rare instances of Robins fighting their own images occur.

David Lack records a Robin that flew at its reflection in his bedroom window. The window was open and the bird used the top of the window as his high perch. The image disappeared and so the owner sang a triumphant song. This bird apparently behaved like this for a fortnight along one side of the house and then stopped — either shattered by his exertions or totally confident that the intruder was not a worthy rival.

Colour preference

Very sophisticated colour preference tests have been devised in the laboratory for many species of bird. These have involved teaching the birds to peck at coloured buttons for food rewards as well as detailed observations on the first pecks made by newly hatched chicks and ducklings. For the Robin's colour preferences we have to rely on the garden experiments carried out in Bristol by Mr Radford in 1969 and 1970.

Mr Radford's garden Robin was in the habit of taking sultanas from his hand. To test the bird's colour preferences he painted some of the sultanas with watercolour paints (red, yellow, green and blue in the first place) and noted whether the bird took natural or coloured fruit when offered the choice of two sultanas at once. The sensible bird took unadulterated sultanas almost every time and had no truck at all with green or blue. Later trials showed that the bird would develop a preference for red fruit after being only offered coloured ones, with natural and yellow fruit second and third. If blue and green only were offered blue was preferred. This demonstrates immediately that Robins are capable of telling one colour from another, just as we can (though many mammals and some birds are unable to do so). The next winter what was probably the same Robin was tested with sultanas painted black or white. Initially black was taken very much more readily than white but, after several more trials, the Robin was quite willing to take white ones.

Of course marking of sultanas with watercolour paint may change their taste and, in any case, experiments on a single bird may not be relevant to all Robins. However the preference for red is very common among birds — Siskins, for example, are particularly fond of taking peanuts from orange plastic feeders in the garden. It is interesting that yellow was the next preferred colour for it is a common colour of many berries — as is black. Some ripe berries are blue but hardly any are green — indeed green berries are usually a sign of unripeness. It i neither in the plant's nor the bird's best interest for young green berries to be eaten. The immature berries will not produce viable seed, nor will they be as nutritious as the ripe ones; so the bird's ability to distinguish and reject green berries is a useful one.

It is possible to set up an experiment in your garden using edible colouring and any sort of food your own Robin will take. The easiest way to do this is to set up two heaps of the differently coloured food and see which (and how many are taken how quickly. Some bait shops actually sell coloured gentles which some Robins like almost as much as mealworms. Beware, though, as your bird may quickly confound your experiment by realizing that all the food is equally good.

Tameness

For the British bird-watcher the Robin is the very epitome of tameness. Of all our bird species it most regularly develops a very strong relationship with man whether as a welcome helper to the gardener or as an honoured guest in the home. This is a trait which is not found in Robin populations elsewhere. In some areas of Europe the Black Redstart breeds within towns and may become almost as tame as the Robin is in Britain. There are no instances of such tameness amongst the rather sparse breeding population of Black Redstarts in Britain.

However, tame Robins have been a feature of British life for many centuries. The earliest record comes from the sixth century at Culross in Fife where St Ser regularly fed a tame Robin. The record of this bird, from a twelfth century account, shows that the saint was very fond of it. St Serf was old at the time an his pupils killed the Robin in a bout of horseplay. They realized that they had done wrong and attempted to divert the blame to one of their number: Kentigern, who was St Serf's favourite. The young boy took up the decapitated body and successfully prayed that it should be restored to life. Kentigern was th grandson of Prince Loth — who gave his name to the Lothians. He was later himself canonized under the name of Mungo — meaning *My Dear One* — whic was bestowed on him by St Serf.

To me the most endearing feature of a Robin's tameness is its continuing independence. There is no way that a tame wild Robin can be considered a pet. The bird's relationship with the human beings in its life does not show the fawning servility of a spoilt lap-dog but is rather that of an independent spirit

which is prepared to 'use' the human to suit itself. We will see elsewhere how much of an imposition the bird may be when it decides to nest in what, for humans, is an inconvenient site. At all times of the year it is, of course, the Robin that chooses to strike up a relationship with man and it will always be the local territory-holding bird that is confident enough to respond to our overtures.

There are essentially two sorts of relationship that are forged. The first occurs when the human tries to gain the Robin's confidence. This is generally possible with patience provided that the circumstances are not against it. For example it is probably impossible to have a hand-tame and house-living Robin if you also have a cat. The Robin can generally be tamed, through a few simple steps, at any time during a cold spell in winter. Some birds may respond at other times: particularly when young birds are setting up their first territories during the autumn. The method relies on feeding the bird and on that magic ingredient – mealworms. I can do no better than quote Lord Grey of Fallodon, the distinguished Edwardian Foreign Secretary, whose tame Robins were famous. He was also a very good field ornithologist and endowed the Edward Grey Institute of Field Ornithology at Oxford. This is from his *The Charm of Birds*:

Any male Robin can be tamed; such at least is my own experience. The bird is first attracted by crumbs of bread thrown on the ground; then a mealworm is thrown to it; then a box – such as one of the small metal boxes in which chemists sell lozenges – is placed open on the ground with mealworms in it. When the bird has become used to this, the next step is to kneel down and place the back of one hand flat upon the ground with the box open on the upturned palm, and the fingers projecting beyond the box. This is the most difficult stage, but Robins will risk their lives for mealworms, and the bird will soon face the fingers and stand on them. The final stage, that of getting the bird to come on the hand when raised above the ground, is easy. The whole process may be a matter of only two or three days in hard weather, when the birds are hungry; and when once it has been accomplished the Robin does not lose its tameness; confidence has been established and does not diminish when weather becomes mild and food plentiful.

It is undoubtedly possible to tame Robins (male or female) without access to a supply of mealworms but they are by far and away the best temptation to put in a Robin's way. Details of how to set up a culture and produce supplies, at home, for even the most voracious Robin, are given on page 106. In any case it is easy to strike up a very happy relationship with one's garden Robin without even approaching the hand-tameness sought by Lord Grey. The occasional pause from digging or hoeing to offer a titbit one has disturbed — for instance a small worm — will often quickly forge a lasting relationship with an individual Robin. It is also possible to use some other sorts of foods for taming the birds: suet, beef fat, dripping and butter are reported as being very good and one bird quickly became addicted to grated mild Cheddar cheese. All these foods are fatty and as such are readily used by the Robin as fuel.

The other type of tame Robin usually attracts our notice during the spring, at the start of the breeding season, and may become a confounded nuisance. This is the bird which decides that a part of someone's house or garden is *the* ideal place to nest. Many people find it hard to be practical and discourage a bird which has appeared to confide in them to the extent to wishing to raise its family close by; however, severe strains can result. Cars have been immobilized by Robins building their nest and rearing their broods in the engine compartment, back-doors rendered unusable by Robin nests in the porch, front doors by nests in letter-boxes and even church music has been silenced for the duration by a nest in the organ bellows! It would often be wrong to describe such birds as being tame but rather they are so strong-willed that they have managed to mould human behaviour to suit their ends.

The Robin's tame behaviour in Britain has a long history following on from the earliest records of St Serf's bird. There are many references to it in literature — particularly poetry — from the Middle Ages to the present day. It seems to be the only species that regularly makes the inside of buildings a part of its territory although others may use buildings in flocks. One of the most famous was the 'Westminster Wonder' which entered and sang in Westminster Abbey in 1695 and took up, as a song post, the catafalque of the dead Queen Mary! Various broadsheets and poems were published to commemorate this event.

Tame Robins indoors have often been associated with ecclesiastical buildings during cold weather. I have been called in to try to catch (humanely) and remove Robins from both a Non-conformist Chapel and a Parish Church (successfully in the former case, unsuccessfully with the latter as the space available for the bird was much too large). The objection, in both cases, was not to the bird's presence *per se* nor to any distraction its winter song caused but simply to the random and inconsiderate distribution of its droppings.

The carefully tamed Robins which accept their food from the hand will often remain to breed in the summer. There are many instances where their mate is brought along for the food too and may also become very tame. However several observers have found that the actual nest site is still a private place and that even mealworms will not be accepted in its close proximity. Lord Grey

The North wind doth blow
And we shall have snow,
And what will the robin do then,
    Poor thing?

He will sleep in the barn
To keep himself warm,
And hide his head under his wing,
    Poor thing!

found that his tame Robin would accept the offering, even close to the nest, but would not feed the food to its nestful of young unless he retreated five or six metres. Others have found that they may be attacked or even postured at, as if they were themselves an intruding Robin (surely the ultimate in acceptance), close to the nest. Later, when the young have fledged, the parent bird (or birds) may bring them along for food and a formal introduction!

In most cases tame Robins remain with their human friends for life. However, there have been cases of quite long interruptions after which the Robin still recognized the human being. For instance in one case the person had left his house, shut up, for six months and, on returning, was greeted by his tame Robin fluttering onto his shoulder. Margaret Nice, working with the American Song Sparrow, had a bird which recognized her after an absence of eighteen months.

The difference between the tame British Robin and its wary Continental counterpart has an interesting consequence. Colonel Meinertzhagen writes that he was able to distinguish the British from the resident Robins on Ushant, off Brittany, when there was an arrival of migrants on September 24th, 1933. This was not only by their subtle colour differences but also because the British birds 'kept close to habitations and showed no fear of man.' The local birds were 'skulkers confined to bush and spinneys away from habitations'. Such differences in behaviour can be seen between populations of birds within a few miles of each other — Woodpigeons in London are tame birds which are easily approached, but in the surrounding countryside only a little distance away they are very shy and wary. In Copenhagen an even more remarkable change comes about in the breeding Greylag Geese on the park lakes. There they will take bread offered by the local residents and yet the very same birds are as wild as any other goose when out feeding on the fields. This population winters in Spain and must be very canny to escape the guns of the French and Spanish wildfowlers on its migrations and during the winter. One hopes that the small proportion of British Robins which do migrate modify their winter behaviour if they choose to stay in areas where the bird-trappers are active.

Hat tame!

Usually the human tamer of a Robin aims to persuade the bird to come to feed on his or her hand. This is not always the case and Mr Wolfendale, the official Watcher for the Royal Society for the Protection of Birds (RSPB) at a sanctuary in Stalybridge, about 40 years ago, trained his birds to feed on his hat (whilst he was wearing it)! It was actually a peaked park-keeper style of cap and the Robins and a Blackbird regularly took food from it.

Mr Wolfendale was able to walk about, use his binoculars and even smoke without disturbing the feeding bird. He describes how he could easily provoke territorial squabbles by placing food on his hat whilst standing in one Robin's territory and then walking into another's. As one would expect, a scrap ensued but the owner of the territory where he was standing would always eventually claim the feeding place. Such

behaviour on the part of the watcher displays true altruism — he would be unable to see the feeding Robin himself but would be a part of the habitat being watched by the human visitors to the sanctuary!

How to breed mealworms

There is no doubt that the way to a Robin's favours is via its stomach and particularly through the temptations provided by mealworms. The mealworm is the larval form of the beetle, *Tenebrio molitor*, and can be reared easily in a box kept in a warm place (the airing cupboard is ideal). The larvae feed on flour, dry porridge oats, stale cornflakes or bread and are odourless if properly kept. They are easy to keep and breed, and well worth it too, because they often sell in pet shops for about the same price the fishmonger charges for best smoked salmon (by weight).

It used to be possible to find pupae with which to start the breeding stock in granaries — where they can be a serious pest — but modern methods of grain storage have largely eliminated infestations. So the initial stock of mealworms will probably have to be bought at a shop specializing in bird foods, though some aquarium suppliers have them too. They are *not* the same as gentles, which are fly maggots that are sold as bait for fishermen and not at all the

same thing. They are a lot cheaper and they (or their pupae) are excellent food for birds, though rather less pleasant to deal with than mealworms (and cannot be raised in the same way).

Your mealworm culture will need a sound home. A full-size biscuit tin is probably the smallest practical container and an old-fashioned enamelled bread-bin is ideal. The larvae and beetles need a medium in the container for them to be able to live and breed. This can be provided by a layer of equal parts of wholemeal flour and porridge oats, about 100cm deep, covered by a layer of bran about 50cm thick. The addition of about 2%, by weight, of dried brewer's yeast to the food layer is said to promote growth and some people add a few cloves, supposedly to speed production, but it will no doubt provide a more exotic flavoured mealworm! The insects need moisture and this is provided by a slice of potato or swede renewed each week. Apart from this the culture must be kept dry or fermentation will take place and the whole lot becomes a bit smelly. It should also, of course, be kept free of other insects. Satisfactory results can also be obtained by using a bed of bran and feeding the mealworms with a slice or two of fresh, damp bread each week. In these circumstances there is no need to add the slice of swede or potato.

The top of the container must be covered with a muslin or mesh covering to stop the inhabitants from escaping. They are best gathered by placing folded sheets of paper on top of the culture as the mealworms will collect in the folds. It would be an unnecessary disturbance to the insects to scrabble through the medium searching for suitable worms. Harvested larvae can be kept for several days, if kept cool, in a small ventilated tin with a little bran in it. Over a period of several months the medium will be reduced to a fine powder and will then need to be renewed.

A culture which is producing well will provide several thousand mealworms a month. Production is speeded up if the tin is kept in a warm place at about 25°C but will slow down or stop if it is allowed to cool. If adult beetles cannot be obtained the culture can be started with mealworms themselves but there will inevitably be a delay whilst they grow into adults and start to breed. This may

delay the production of mealworms by a couple of months or so.

Although this culture is being recommended for the sake of the Robins in particular, many other species will greatly relish the mealworms. Tits are very partial to them at all times of the year and they can be fed even at the height of the breeding season without fear of harming the young birds. Mealworms are also very useful if you have to look after sick or injured birds. They provide an immediately available and acceptable food for the tricky insectivorous species of bird. It is as well to remember that they do seem to be a particularly rich food and some individual birds that feed too much on mealworms may suffer from an upset digestion!

Caring for Robins

Anyone interested in birds will, now and again, come across sick or injured birds and, if neighbours know of their interest, they will get small boxes with 'patients' brought to their door. Dealing with victims that happen to be Robins is no different from treating other mainly insectivorous small birds. Generally long-term care should be left to an expert and there are usually skilled volunteers providing a Bird Hospital service somewhere locally. It is possible to get in touch with them through the RSPCA, a local vet or even the Public Library.

Any treatment should be directed, as its ultimate aim, to the release of a healthy bird to the wild. Even if the bird has a broken leg or other serious injury recovery is often possible and birds with healed beaks, even amputated legs, have survived well and reared young. The first rule is *never* to take into care a very young bird that has just left the nest, where there is any chance of releasing it where it was found. The vast majority of such nestlings never were abandoned and would have had a much better chance of surviving in the care of their parents than of some human. It may seem callous to put it back but it is certainly the best thing to do — even if there is a risk of cat predation. Parents may reappear after an absence of several hours. Truly orphaned chicks, in or out of the nest, require special treatment and are probably best taken to an expert.

Most birds you have to treat will have suffered traumatic injury of some sort. Often they will have been rescued from a cat, hit by a car or flown against a window. If they are wet they will need to be dried using absorbent tissues or even a hair-dryer (not too hot and not too close). Any bleeding will probably have stopped but, if the wound is fresh, a tissue pad gently applied to the site of the bleeding should do the trick. Then, in most circumstances, an insensible or dopey bird should be put in a small cardboard box, with soft-bedding and air-holes, and kept in a warm, dark place for several hours without any attempt being made to feed or water it. If the bird is very obviously seriously wounded then expert help should be sought but, believe it or not, many casualties recover in a few hours (or overnight) and will fly away when you open the box. Do not open it indoors if you think there is any chance of the bird flying — it could well kill itself against a window.

The main problems with birds that have to be kept longer are how to house them and what to give them to eat. The first thought may be an old budgie cage for a home — quite acceptable for a short-stay patient — but it must be housed somewhere that is undisturbed and warm. Food for a bird like a Robin can include all sorts of insect food that is produced commercially for fish — *dehydrated food must be moistened* — as well as special softbill bird foods (to the bird fancier a softbill is any insectivorous songbird) available from petshops. Mealworms, gentles, small worms from the garden (redworms from the compost heap are excellent), mashed up hard-boiled egg, cooked fat from the Sunday joint — all will be taken and variety is excellent for the bird. Feed small amounts often; not too much at one go.

The one obvious serious injury that can be readily treated is a broken tarsus (lower part of the leg). This can be set with a pair of improvised splints and sellotape to hold them in place. The break may heal in as little as ten days.

Some accidents are, of course, avoidable with a little foresight. For instance many birds of all species, particularly juveniles, fly into windows — sometimes they just knock themselves out but they can often be killed. Obscuring the window with curtains or hanging plants can help but a really good system is to hang a cut-out of a flying Sparrowhawk in the window.

Cats are often a problem to Robins although they are supposed not to like the taste of Robin flesh. Although some cat repellents do work (particularly the permanent ones), I consider that the best defence against cat problems in many suburban gardens is to have one's own! At least then it is likely to make your garden its territory and not let all your neighbouring hunting moggies in.

If cats are a problem it is up to you to make sure that your feeding station does not encourage the feeding birds to come within reach of a waiting cat. It is also a good idea for you to try to provide safe nesting places for your Robins that the cats cannot get to. A means of doing this (and keeping out grey squirrels) is to surround the nest-site with 2" mesh wire netting — the birds will not mind but the predators should not be able to get through. Of course the Robin can sometimes itself provide its own defence: I have heard of gardens where the breeding Robin makes the life of the owner's cat a total misery during the breeding season!

Captive breeding

Robin Redbreast in a cage
Sets all Heaven in a rage

Although the very idea of keeping Robins in captivity will nauseate many readers there are some aviculturalists who are obsessed with the challenge of getting different species of bird to breed in captivity. For some species this can be genuinely beneficial to their conservation, for the captive-bred offspring may satisfy any demand there is for them as caged birds, removing the desire to go out and capture fresh wild ones. Also, if the species concerned is very rare, young from captive pairs might provide birds for release into the wild to help build up natural populations. In any case such dedicated bird fanciers tend to provide palatial surroundings for their birds and look after them with tender loving care.

In Victorian times there was a claimed successful breeding of a Robin in an aviary but other keepers failed to get Robins in their care even to pair. During David Lack's studies he was able to induce two captive pairs to raise full clutches of five young. The birds were caught after they had paired and each of two large aviaries, extensively planted with natural vegetation, had two pairs of Robins placed in them. In each it was only the dominant pair that nested and, almost always, only the cock of the dominant pair that sang. In fact the cock in one of the aviaries managed to hold sway over an area outside it which he could never visit! The young were fed mainly on huge numbers of mealworms provided for the parents and, as soon as they had properly fledged, the families were released. The captive breeding experiment had been conducted to find out some of the more intimate details of their behaviour.

The other two captive breeding attempts relate to hand-reared birds from wild nests that had met with a disaster. In 1968 Colin Harrison took over two young from one nest and a single youngster from another. They were kept in small compartments in his greenhouse during the winter. It quickly became clear that the singleton had little realization that it was a bird, let alone a Robin, but thought it was a person! However the other two behaved like Robins and seemed to be male and female. When, in spring, one started to show signs of nest-building, they were transferred to a bigger compartment divided down the middle – in case they should fight each other. Towards the end of March the division was removed and Colin had managed to duplicate the amalgamation of neighbouring territories, on a small scale, that sometimes happens when wild birds pair up. These birds reared young to eight days old, when they were found dead outside the nest. It was suggested that the male was the culprit and that, at the stage when the chicks started to grow feathers and become recognizable as birds, his aggression got the better of him. In the wild the male would have been defending his territory against other Robins and would also have had to spend a great deal of time finding the food which, in captivity, was served up on a plate!

The next year Frank Meaden successfully bred Robins in his aviaries at Cheshunt. The two birds had come from different orphaned nests and were kept through the winter in adjacent enclosures. The two birds were allowed to come together on April 1st and the hen was sitting on five eggs by the 10th. Four young left the nest but one drowned in a pond. Seventeen days later the male attacked and killed one of his chicks and beat up another – this and the unharmed one were removed from the aviary. When the second clutch hatched it became clear that the male had become aggressive just when the female started to incubate their second clutch of eggs.

It therefore seems possible, with a great deal of care, to breed Robins in captivity. It may also be an interesting and rewarding pastime for anyone who is looking after orphaned Robins which cannot, for some reason, be released to the wild. But it seems likely that any attempt in a small aviary may be troubled by unusual behaviour. David Lack's birds were kept in aviaries of 30 sq.m or more when their apparently natural breeding took place.

Exploitation

The very thought of human exploitation of Robins in Britain at the present time is almost unthinkable. The birds have been protected by a ban on killing, egg collecting or caging by law for many years and, in most areas, long before legal protection was introduced, by local custom. This was not always the case and in parts of Southern Europe Robins were still caught and caged, or even eaten, regularly until very recently.

Apart from the ritual killing of a very few Robins during 'hunts' (see page 124) there is some evidence that a small number were taken for food in Britain: there is an Elizabethan reference stating that 'Robin redbreasts are esteemed a light and good meat!' However the recipes for cooking Robins in English books all

*Song contests between birds have often been staged by bird keepers –
teaching the bird to sing what the judges may want can be a long, tedious
job!*

seem to have come from France. There the large numbers of migrant Robins
would be much easier to catch in quantity and also fatter.

The unfortunate Robin had a reputation in Britain, as did almost every
creature, as a physic. The powdered ashes of a burnt Robin were an ingredient
in medicines for the removal of bladder stones and curing of epilepsy. Robin
droppings, taken internally with other ingredients, were a specific against a
runny tummy (though perhaps more likely to cause one). Externally, they were
said to be a cure for scurf, sunburn and freckles – this last surely a case of the
cure being worse than the complaint!

The caging of live Robins as songbirds in Britain was not very usual but still
quite widespread until the beginning of this century. Young birds caught in the
summer, still in juvenile plumage, were recommended. They were called 'greys'
and were settled in their cages so that they could moult through into the adult
plumage: then they would sing through the autumn and winter. One
recommendation was that three or four 'greys' should be purchased and caged
separately and out of each other's sight but within hearing. Their efforts at song
would reinforce one another and so at least one excellent songster should result.
Another recommendation was to hang the cages one above the other at
Christmas time. This author (William Kidd), writing in the middle of the last
century, urges the keepers of Robins to talk, sing and whistle at them to
encourage them to sing. His section on the species ends by discouraging their
caging: 'A garden is the proper place to court the society of Master Bob, or a
country lane. Here, in the autumn, he is in all his glory.' It was quite possible for
Robins to be taught the song of other species by exposing the young birds to it
whilst they were still 'greys'. Several remarkable birds have been reported which
were raised with (or by) Nightingales – some sang as well as their foster
parents.

There was certainly a small but regular a trade in caged Robins at this time. Mayhew, in 1851, gave the price of a 'grey' as a shilling but a whole pound sterling for a bird in adult plumage, caged and singing. He thought that about 3,000 were sold each year with a third dying in the process. This was very much lower than the huge totals for the more popular finches. The Robins were even then not always easy to sell because of the popular belief that caging them was likely to bring bad luck. Further exploitation came with the fashions for egg collecting: several suppliers would offer clutches of blown eggs in their catalogues and there was even a short period when Robin skins were used in the millinery trade as ornamentation for ladies' hats.

On the Continent Robins used to be eaten in large numbers during the migration season and, in the south, during the winter. Migrating Robins will often put on a great deal of weight and, so we are told, the fatter birds make better eating. The migrants are also much more likely to be caught in numbers and, in some wintering areas, they may also be very common. In some cases the reported numbers caught may well indicate that, in these areas, there may be many wandering birds which are non-territorial. Travellers in Italy have remarked on the huge numbers of dead Robins offered for sale in the food markets — horrified Englishmen have often been assured that they are very 'sweet meat'.

In France, Italy and Algeria the birds used to be caught very easily on sticks smothered with gooey birdlime placed round a decoy. The decoy will sometimes have been a caged Robin but by far the best results came from limed sticks placed round a captive Little Owl on a swivel perch. Once the first Robin had seen the owl it immediately approached to mob the bird and would generally get stuck on a lime twig. In struggling to free itself the frantic bird would utter the high intensity alarm call and attract all the other Robins within earshot. By shifting the owl on its perch from place to place an experienced trapper working his Italian patch could kill over 100, even 200, Robins during the course of single day spent trapping.

This unfortunate Robin is not engaging in acrobatics but is caught on a lime stick. In Europe liming is now particularly associated with Cyprus but it may be used (by illegal bird-catchers) even in Britain.

Robins and the law

The first legal protection in Britain afforded to Robins was in 1872 when they were listed (as Robin Redbreast) in the Wild Birds Protection Act and so were partly protected during the close season: this ran from March 14th to August 1st. Over the next eighty years legal protection for the Robin gradually improved: in particular the most barbarous trapping methods were proscribed.

Under the 1954 Act the Robin itself received full protection throughout the year but, through a general reluctance to make schoolboy egg collecting an offence, it was not forbidden to take the eggs of Robins and 21 other common species. On St Valentine's Day, 1963, after the very cold winter had caused massive mortality among most resident species, Lord Hurcomb successfully asked the Government to close this loophole.

The Wildlife and Countryside Act, 1981, is the current protection Act covering England, Scotland and Wales. Under it all Robins, their eggs and nests, are protected at all times of the year. Birds may be caught (ringed and released) by licensed ringers, they may be taken or killed if they are endangering human life, spreading disease or doing serious damage to crops, etc. Anyone may care for (or humanely destroy) any injured Robin that they encounter – provided that the injury was not caused through 'their unlawful act'. It is also not an offence to collect feathers, wings, feet, skulls (or even whole birds) from road casualties or other bodies found in the countryside or along the tide-line. Taking eggs from a nest, even one that has certainly been deserted, is always an offence and anyone with eggs of wild birds in their possession should be able to prove that they have not been illegally taken.

Prosecutions relating to Robins are uncommon. The RSPB investigations department had one case that involved 75 finches and a Robin caged in Peckham, just before Christmas 1980, where the defendant was eventually fined £50 with £200 costs. This case was taken more than a hundred years after the species was first protected by law. Anyone who suspects that an offence has been committed involving wild birds should contact the RSPB investigations section (phone 0767-80551); they are experts who deal with bird law all the time; you would have to be lucky to find a bird expert on your local police force.

As you will appreciate, the protection in law provided to Robins is quite good, but do not get worried that ordinary responsible birdwatchers run the risk of prosecution. It is not an offence to look at a Robin's nest (but do be careful) nor to photograph the bird at the nest; if the Robin were really rare, it would be added to a special schedule of the Wildlife and Countryside Act so that a licence would be required even for watching it at the nest. It is quite nice to think that the deliberations of MPs and peers over the years have not been solely concerned with the national debt, income tax and school meals, but have also made life in Britain better for all species of bird.

What's in a name?

The very special relationship that we have built up with our Robins in Britain is reflected in the bird's name. Robin is actually an affectionate nickname associated with two favourites of legend – Robin Hood and Robin Goodfellow.

In fact the bird we know as the Robin has the scientific name *Erithacus rubecula*. The first (generic) name is derived from the Greek name for the bird – *erithakos* – which in turn is derived from *erythros* which means 'red'. The specific name – *rubecula* – means 'little red one'. Obviously the red breast of the Robin is the immediate feature by which it has been named in almost every country. In Britain the Anglo-Saxon name was *Ruddoc* and 'Ruddock' or 'Reddock' may still be in use in some country areas. In the Middle Ages 'Redbreast' was used and in the fifteenth or sixteenth century the petname of 'Robin Redbreast' came into use. The use of Robin, by itself, is relatively recent and most people would have spoken of the bird as a Redbreast until a few decades ago. In 1952 the British Ornithologist's Union List officially accepted Robin as the correct name.

Unusually, for such a familiar and common bird, there are not many local names recorded for the Robin. In Gaelic it is known as *Broindergh*, meaning 'red belly', and in Welsh as *Yr hobel goch*, meaning 'red bird'. There are also some places where it has been called the 'Ploughman's Bird': presumably because the local Robin will have been as familiar to the horse or ox ploughman slowly turning the furrows as it is now to the gardener digging with a spade or fork.

The nickname Robin has been further shortened in some parts of the country to 'Bob' and there are many instances of 'Robinet' being used. This is a diminutive of a diminutive and was also applied to a small gun called a culverin in Elizabethan times, which took a small load of a pound or less. However David Lack discovered that there were other sizes of gun also named after birds but, in all cases, these were birds of prey. It is therefore more likely that the Robin after which the gun was named was the male Hobby. This small migrant falcon was named, by the falconers 'Robin', on account of its russet belly and trousers.

In Europe the Robin has not become a tame bird of gardens as it has in Britain and so all the European names reflect the bird's distinctive red breast and no nickname has gained general usage. If you open up one of the popular field guides the following four names are given:

Roodborst	Dutch	*Rotkehlchen*	German
Rougegorge	French	*Rödhake*	Swedish

These all clearly describe the bird and there are a large number of other examples from all over the Continent.

Britain's national bird

The International Council for Bird Preservation (ICBP), at a meeting in Tokyo during 1960, asked its various national sections to choose national birds. The British section took its responsibility very seriously and the Chairman, Lord Hurcomb, wrote to The Times on October 18th, 1960, and the resulting correspondence and consultation was used to decide the matter.

From the start there were only two serious contenders: the Red Grouse – since, at that time, it was considered a separate species from the Willow Grouse and so was the only full species found exclusively in Britain and Ireland – and the Robin. It fairly quickly became clear that the Robin was the favourite for a very wide range of people and it was announced as Britain's National Bird in a letter to The Times on December 15th. There can be few, if

any, who would question the wisdom of the decision – now immortalized in the logo of the British Section of the ICBP by Robert Gillmor.

Babes in the wood

One of the best-known stories about the Robin is the covering of the dead bodies of the Babes in the Wood. Although the story has all the ingredients of an ancient folk-tale, modified for the nursery, the earliest reference so far found of this behaviour in print comes from four hundred years ago: 'A Robbyn read breast, fynding the dead body of a Man or a Woman, wyll couer the face of the same with Mosse. And as some holdes opinion, he wyll couer also the whole body.'

This is from A Thousand Notable Things of Sundrie Sorts by Thomas Lupton, a book which contains an amazing assortment of specious sayings, mostly garnered from other works. Many came from the classics but there is no indication that this particular item was anything but recent. David Lack was unable to find any evidence for an earlier source.

As far as the main story of the Babes in the Wood goes, various broadsheets and poems relate the same sort of tale. In it a Norfolk gentleman, on his deathbed, commends his two children into the care of his brother as he and his wife are both dying. The children are left a very handsome sum of money kept for them till they grow up. However the wicked uncle hires a couple of ruffians to take the children

away and kill them. Refusing to do the dastardly deed, one ruffian kills the other and then abandons the children in a large deserted wood. In the original story the children eventually die:

> *Thus wandered these poor*
>   *innocents,*
> *Till death did end their grief;*
> *In one another's arms they died,*
>   *As wanting due relief;*
> *No burial this pretty pair*
>   *From any man receives,*
> *Till robin redbreast piously*
>   *Did cover them with leaves.*

In the present day pantomime the outcome for the wicked uncle is just as bad as the original but the babes are actually rescued by, of all people, Robin Hood.

It seems very likely that the story relates to a ballad or, just possibly, a real event from the sixteenth century. Most of the earlier versions specifically mention Norfolk but in others the county is Northamptonshire or Nottinghamshire. When David Lack went to Norfolk and asked about the story in 1948 the very wood was pointed out to him (Wayland Wood near Watton). This was associated with the story as early as 1739 but, as he pointed out, the Doone Valley on Exmoor postdates the novel Lorna Doone.

Nursery rhymes

Apart from *Babes in the Wood* with the episode relating to the Robin and the sagas of 'The Marriage of Cock Robin and Jenny Wen' and 'The Death and Burial of Cock Robin' there are several nursery rhymes about the Robin. Some children's verses are almost certainly of fairly recent origin but others may date back a very long time. For instance the Robin was Thor's bird and the Hazel was Thor's tree. A game called 'Robin's alight' was played in Cornwall and Scotland: one hopes not by children. A lighted hazel twig was passed from hand to hand, being continually twirled, the person holding the stick when the flame went out had to pay a forfeit. Perhaps there is an echo of this in:

Little Bob Robin,
Where do you live?
Up in yonder wood, sir,
On a hazel twig.

Other short verses were obviously repeated by mothers to get their young babies
to take an interest in their surroundings. For instance:

Little Robin Redbreast
Sat upon a rail;
Niddle noddle went his head,
Wiggle waggle went his tail.

Possibly some faulty natural history here, but a satisfactory bit of doggerel for
the child. An autumn visit of a Robin within church is celebrated in the
following — good advice too from more than 400 years ago.

Robin redbreast with his notes
Singing aloft in the quire,
Warneth to get you frieze coats,
For Winter then draweth near.

Finally there was a children's round game, almost certainly of great antiquity,
which survived until just over a hundred years ago.

Cock Robin is dead and gone to his grave,
H'm, haw, gone to his grave.
Cock Robin is dead and gone to his grave,
H'm, haw, gone to his grave.

There grew an old apple-tree over his head,
H'm, haw, over his head.
There grew an old apple-tree over his head,
H'm, haw, over his head.

The apples were ripe and they all fell down,
H'm, haw, they all fell down.
The apples were ripe and they all fell down,
H'm, haw, they all fell down.

There came an old woman a-picking 'em up,
H'm, haw, picking 'em up.
There came an old woman a-picking 'em up,
H'm, haw, picking 'em up.

Old Robin arose and gave her a knock,
H'm, haw, gave her a knock.
Old Robin arose and gave her a knock,
H'm, haw, gave her a knock.

Which made the old woman go hippity hop,
H'm, haw, hippity hop!
Which made the old woman go hippity hop,
H'm, haw, hippity hop!

Who killed Cock Robin?

The best known poem about Robins, indeed of any involving birds, is undoubtedly 'Who killed Cock Robin?' or, more properly, 'The Death and Burial of Cock Robin'. It was a sequel to another, very similar epic 'The Marriage of Cock Robin and Jenny Wren'.

The two poems are thought of now as simple children's verses of no particular significance. Indeed they seem to lack any real moral – and this points to their antiquity. It would have been unthinkable for a Georgian or Victorian writer to compose a series of verses for children without very obvious praise of good deeds and good morality. In fact the earliest printed copies are from about 250 years ago but there are various indications that the rhymes were handed down by word of mouth from much earlier. For instance the marriage of the Robin and the Wren brings to mind the ancient rituals performed by Celtic people.

Some more modern versions of the verses exist where there are references to political events but most versions are surprisingly similar. They have been collected from all over Britain and from most areas that have been settled by the British. David Lack consulted many different printed sources before producing the definitive versions of the two poems, as they would have been related in the early part of the eighteenth century. The 'Marriage' runs to 36 verses and the 'Death' to 14 of four lines each.

The Death and Burial of Cock Robin

Who killed Cock Robin?
  I said the Sparrow,
  With my bow and arrow,
And I killed Cock Robin.

Who did see him die?
  I, said the Fly,
  With my little eye,
And I saw him die.

Who catched his blood?
  I, said the Fish,
  With my little dish,
And I catched his blood.

Who made his shroud?
  I, said the Beetle,
  With my little needle,
And I made his shroud.

Who shall dig his grave?
  I, says the Owl,
  With my spade and showl,
And I will dig his grave.

Who will be the parson?
  I, says the Rook,
  With my little book,
And I will be the parson.

Who will be the clerk?
  I, says the Lark,
  If 'tis not in the dark,
And I will be the clerk.

Who'll carry him to the grave?
  I, says the Kite,
  If 'tis not in the night,
And I'll carry him to the grave.

Who will carry the link,
  I, says the Linnet,
I'll fetch it in a minute,
And I will carry the link.

Who will be chief mourner?
  I, says the Dove,
  For I mourn for my love,
And I'll be the chief mourner.

Who will bear the pall?
  We, says the Wren
  Both the cock and the hen,
And we will bear the pall.

Who will sing a psalm?
  I, says the Thrush,
  As she sat in a bush,
And I will sing a psalm.

Who will toll the bell?
  I, says the Bull,
  Because I can pull,
And so Cock Robin farewell.

All the birds of the air
  Fell to sighing and sobbing
  When they heard the bell toll
For poor Cock Robin.

Various parts of this are of particular interest. The use of 'showl' (shovel) to rhyme with owl shows an early origin: 'showl' is an archaic version of shovel (modern versions may substitute the word 'trowel'). By the time the printed versions were set down kites were beginning to retreat to their current small breeding area in Wales — earlier they would have been a very familiar sight even in cities. The 'link' that the Linnet was going to carry was a flaming torch which, in some parts of the country, was a part of the funeral procession even in daylight. Finally the Bull who is to toll the bell is very likely to have been a Bullfinch — they were often caged and given toy bells to play with.

An amusing 'reconstruction' of Cock Robin's funeral was arranged by the Victorian taxidermist Walter Potter and exhibited at his museum at Bramber in Sussex. It is now (1984), with other parts of his collection, at the Museum of Curiosities in Arundel. The tableau features 96 British birds, many with glass tears in their eyes; the newly dug grave is littered with the bones of previous occupants and the whole *extraordinary affair continues to amuse visitors.*

The 'Marriage' is too long to give here in its entirety. However, in defence of the Sparrow, who is nowadays generally thought of as the murderer, the last four stanzas are reproduced to show that this was not the case. The wedding feast was in full swing with all the birds singing fit to burst:

> When in came the Cuckoo,
>   And made a great rout;
> He caught hold of Jenny,
>   And pulled her about.
>
> Cock Robin was angry,
>   And so was the Sparrow,

> Who now is preparing his
>   Bow and his arrow.
>
> His aim he took,
>   But he took it not right;
> His skill it was bad,
>   Or his shot in a fright;
>
> For the Cuckoo he missed,
>   But Cock Robin he killed!
> And all the birds mourned
>   That his blood was so spilled.

Thus, whatever one's sentiments about Sparrows, the verdict would have to be 'Death by misadventure' and not murder.

Wassail

In many parts of Britain, particularly in the south west, the wassailing of the cider-apple orchards was a regular ritual at the beginning of the year. It gave a good excuse for the consumption of a great deal of cider, whilst having the declared aim of promoting a good crop for the next year. The date most normally chosen was December 26th but, in some areas, January 6th (Christmas day before the adjustment of the calendar in 1752) was still used as late as 1930.

The drinking was carried out in the orchard round a large fire. During the evening, whilst a local variant of the wassail song was sung, shot guns were fired into the branches of the trees to scare away the bad spirits — bringers of disease and crop failure. The good spirits had to be tempted to stay in the orchard and so, since they were believed to be embodied in the Robins, slices of toasted bread dipped in cider were poked amongst the branches to encourage the birds to stay.

Robin cards

The Robin is the most familiar creature on cards at Christmas. We are so used to this now, that it comes as a surprise to discover that Robins are not mentioned in the Bible and in fact don't even occur in the Holy Land. Generally, nowadays, the bird is depicted in a snowy scene with other symbols of Christmas such as holly and mistletoe. The holly and the mistletoe have pagan religious significance but the Robin is there for two unconnected reasons.

To the designers of cards it is now traditional to depict the Robin and, if there needs to be an additional reason, the happy relationship between man and bird, particularly in the winter, seems to be quite sufficient. However, the earliest cards came into being in the middle of the last century when cheap colour printing by various processes had just become possible and the 'Penny post' was available to all. The first cards were really very similar to some of the more traditional-looking designs which continue to be used now. They make clear the real reason for the Robin being present: the bird represents the postman!

When the early cards were produced the standard uniform for a postman included, as its most obvious component, a bright red coat. This was readily connected with the bird — the redbreast — and so the standard nickname for the postman became redbreast or Robin. Both names are to be found in novels of the time including *Framley Parsonage* by Anthony Trollope. The book was actually published in 1861, which happens to be the year that the standard uniform was changed: the coat became blue but still had red facings. Trollope was, himself, working in the Post Office as a travelling inspector whilst writing his novels and is credited with invention of the pillar-box: also bright red.

A further reason for choosing the Robin may have been the legend that the red on its breast was caused by the bird being pierced by a thorn from Jesus's crown when He was on the cross. This is basically a Breton legend and does not seem to have a very long history in Britain. However, it was during the mid-Victorian times that there was a great flowering of interest in folklore and the legend had certainly been published in Britain by the time the Christmas card Robins started to be printed.

The postman explanation seems to be much more likely as so many of the very earliest cards show the Robin at the door. Some have the bird actually knocking, others have envelopes in their beaks. The most elaborate ones even have tiny folded letters dangling from fine threads in the bird's beak. When opened, they read 'A Merry Christmas' and 'A Happy New Year' respectively. For me the absolute clincher for the theory that the Robin on our cards originated as the postman is a Valentine Card with exactly the same sort of design: the message dangling from the bird's beak reads 'I Love You'.

We certainly do not, nowadays, imagine that the Robins on our Christmas cards have anything to do with the postman. Robins in snow have become accepted as an integral part of Christmas and are sure to remain so. Their Yuletide presence is by no means confined to cards and they are also familiar in the home on wrapping paper, crackers and even cake decorations. The image of the red-breasted Robin is also used in countless advertisements and window displays, even, in some towns and cities, as huge illuminated images.

There were some examples of exceptionally bad taste displayed on early cards. One showed a Robin about to enter a lethal birdcatcher's trap — not the most pleasant image for Christmas. The explanation seems to have been that the card was printed in Germany and the printer gave his English customer a standard Robin picture from a local bird book. In the last years of the Victorian era very ostentatious cards were produced with real feathers being used for the Robins — indeed Professor Newton complained that Robins were actually killed for use on cards. It is thought that this was not very common, for David Lack was unable to find any that had survived to recent times.

Lest it be thought that this is a one-way exploitation of the Robin by man, there are some happy consequences for the birds. I am sure the presence of all the Robins on cards must remind a few people who would otherwise have forgotten to put the remnants of the Christmas turkey carcase out for the birds when it has been finished with.

Folklore

There are many legends associated with birds throughout the world. The most ancient for the Robin may be its reputation as a fire-bringer. The origins of the legend probably go right back to prehistoric times when man was very dependent on fire. In some stories the Robin in the legend is the sole fetcher of the fire, as for example on Guernsey, in others the Robin is part of a relay of birds who pass the flaming brand from one to the other. In the Breton version of the tale the Wren passes it to the Robin who passes it to the Lark which finally brings it to earth.

There may be an obvious association between the red on the bird's breast and the red of the flame, but the other species associated with fire-bringing is the Wren, which is completely lacking in red on the plumage. Possibly both species may have been linked, at nesting time, with piles of dry sticks collected for the fire. It may even be that the dry nest material from an old Wren or Robin nest, both of which are frequently stuffed into a dry nook or cranny, was used as tinder in emergency.

Very old rituals have been associated with these legends. They involve Wren (or Robin) hunts which seem to have been common in many of the Celtic countries, the object being to catch and kill the bird. The rituals have survived into the twentieth century in the Isle of Man and Ireland as well as a very few places in England, Scotland and France. They would now be illegal under EEC regulations of course.

Another variation of the fire-bringing legend is that the Robin got its red breast from being singed whilst it was trying to quench the fires of hell. There are versions like this recorded from Sweden, France and particularly Wales. There the Robin was sometimes called *Bronrhuddyn* which means 'scorched breast' to commemorate these heroic acts which it is supposed to repeat every day. The Welsh version has been put into verse:

> 'Nay,' said Grandmother, 'have you not heard,
> My poor bad boy, of the fiery pit,
> And how drop by drop this merciful bird
> Carries the water that quenches it?
>
> He brings cool dew in his little bill
> And lets it fall on the souls of men;
> You can see the marks on his red breast still
> Of the fires that scorch as he drops it in.

Later associations with Christ connect the red on the bird's breast with the crown of thorns. In some the Robin is stained by Christ's blood whilst trying to remove the crown, in others the blood is far from the bird which has been pierced by one of the thorns. For example:

124

Bearing His cross, while Christ passed forth forlorn,
His God-like forehead by the mock crown torn,
A little bird took from that crown one thorn
To soothe the dear Redeemer's throbbing head.

This was written in about 1600 by John Hoskyns. Once more the Robin and the Wren are associated in the rhyme, known in many different versions from most parts of the country:

Robins and wrens
Are God Almighty's friends,
Martins and swallers
Are God Almighty's scholars.

The association with Christ crucified and the bird's general tameness have also given rise to many superstitions foretelling disaster if a Robin is harmed. It is possible that these may result from even earlier associations: the Robin was Thor's bird in the Norse mythology. Any Viking harming a Robin or its nest was expected to have his home destroyed by fire or lightning or his cows to give bloody milk.

The punishments to be expected in Britain by the person who had harmed a Robin have been very varied. An attack of bloody milk might still be expected in some areas, in others the household crockery would be smashed, the person perpetrating the deed might suffer an epileptic fit or, in parts of Ireland, a lump would form on the right hand. There were therefore various warning verses:

The robin and the lintil,   or   He that hurts robin or wren
The laverock and the wren,   Will never prosper, boy nor man.
Them that harries their nest
Will never thrive again.

The 'lintil' and the 'laverock' are Scots names for the Linnet and Skylark. Finally the Robin has also entered Suffolk folklore as a weather forecaster.

If the Robin sings in the bush,
Then the weather will be coarse;
But if the robin sings on the barn,
Then the weather will be warm.

This displays a completely pessimistic opinion of Suffolk weather and an indifference to poetical niceties such as accurate rhyming. It is also somewhat distant from true life, as the Robin habitually sings from within a bush and very seldom from an exposed site. Eric Simms recorded the position of hundreds of singing Robins during the 1950s at Dollis Hill, North London. Less than ten times were buildings used — the birds were almost invariably in bushes or trees.

125

Amateur research

Many amateur birdwatchers have contributed to the study of Robins through publishing their observations in the pages of *British Birds* and other journals. A few have gone on to carry out detailed studies of Robin populations in their area. A huge debt is owed to the amateur members of the British Trust for Ornithology who year after year gather vital information on Robins, and many other species, through the network research organized by the BTO. 'Network research' is simply a term used to cover the organized gathering of many individual observations to make a coherent whole.

The longest running operation is the National Bird Ringing Scheme, which started 75 years ago – well before the BTO was founded in 1933. Properly trained bird ringers, licensed through the Nature Conservancy Council, have marked over 15 million birds in Britain since then. Almost a third of a million of these have been found later – usually by ordinary members of the public who have found the birds, either dead or wounded, read the return address on the ring and reported the unique serial numbers. Everyone can help by checking every bird they find dead for a ring. If you find one send it in (writing the number on the letter as well) with details of the find (place, date, circumstances) to the BTO and we will let you know where it was ringed. The information is used both to plot movements and to work out mortality and population parameters.

Interested birdwatchers can also learn to become ringers themselves. Training programmes are arranged by experienced local ringers during the normal course of their ringing activities (often at weekends) and will take two or three years. A few people who start to ring find that the necessary skills are beyond them and very few, including at least two active and fully-trained ringers, find that they are allergic to living birds and have to give up.

Secondly there is a dedicated band of nest recorders who regularly fill in cards (see p. 78) for all the nests that they find. This gives us vital information on the productivity of the birds each year. New contributors to this scheme, even if they only expect to be able to complete cards for a couple of dozen nests of common species each year, are very welcome.

Finally there is a dedicated corps of field-workers who do the Common Birds Census each spring and early summer. This involves regular visits to plot, on a large-scale map, the birds that have taken up territories within the area being surveyed. Eight or more detailed visits are needed and the observations have to be made according to strict rules. Help is needed with different sorts of plot in different parts of the country – farmland in many areas, particular sorts of woodland in others. Experienced birdwatchers who want to help should write to find out the sort of site on which work is needed near their home.

Full details of these schemes and of membership of the BTO are available from the HQ: Beech Grove, Station Road, Tring, Herts HP23 5NR.

Further reading

The classic Robin book is David Lack's *The Life of the Robin* which was first published in 1943, by Witherby, with a revised Pelican edition published in 1953 by Penguin. Less well known is David Lack's other book, *Robin Redbreast*, published by Oxford University Press in 1950 which deals in more detail with the literature and legend of the bird. Robins in gardens feature in *The Garden Bird Book* edited by David Glue (Macmillan 1982, paperback 1984) and facts and figures about Robins and many other species appear in *Enjoying Ornithology*, edited by Ron Hickling (Poyser, 1983). Many notes and articles on Robins have (and will) appear in the periodical literature, particularly:

British Birds, Fountains, Park Lane, Blunham, Bedford MK44 3NJ.

Bird Study, British Trust for Ornithology, Beech Grove, Tring, Herts HP23 5NR.

Ibis, British Ornithologists' Union, c/o Zoological Society, Regents Park, London NW1 4RY.

All Robin enthusiasts wishing to enter more fully into their bird's life will also eagerly await the scientific monograph being prepared by David Harper for publication by Cambridge University Press within the next year or two.

Index (prepared by Jill Graves)